"Andrew is great showing you a peak into what it's like being in a professional touring band with tons of humor, candor, self-depreciation and harsh realities. I felt like I was in the van again with a bunch of smelly men. Thank God that's over."
—BRUCE FITZHUGH
Living Sacrifice

"Andrew Schwab invites you on the Project 86 tour bus in his great new book *It's All Downhill From Here: On the Road With Project 86.* Never a dull moment as Andrew shares all the challenges, the craziness and ultimately those magical moments of being in a touring band. Check it out."
—BRANDON EBEL
President, Tooth and Nail Records

"In *It's All Downhill From Here,* Schwab uses his writing as both a personal therapeutic method of venting emotion, as well as an extremely interesting and humorous means of entertainment. His bluntness is extraordinary, and his willingness to say those things that no one wants to say should secure his place as one of the most honest lyricists in this era of music."
—BRANDON RIKE
Vocalist, Dead Poetic

"This book is completely biased and should not be released. Andrew makes no effort to tell our side of the story and we, his bandmates, are furious. TALK TO MY ATTORNEY, ANDREW."
—RANDY TORRES
Project 86

IT'S ALL DOWNHILL FROM HERE

ON THE ROAD WITH PROJECT 86

BY LEAD VOCALIST

ANDREW SCHWAB

[RELEVANTBOOKS]

Published by Relevant Books

A division of Relevant Media Group, Inc.

www.relevant-books.com

www.relevantmediagroup.com

Cover Design by Don Clark

Interior Design by Joshua Smith and Jeremy Kennedy

Interior Photography Courtesy of Randy Torres and Katie Peligrino

Library of Congress Control Number: 2004093616

International Standard Book Number: 0-9746942-9-0

For information or bulk orders:

RELEVANT MEDIA GROUP, INC.

POST OFFICE BOX 951127

LAKE MARY, FL 32795

407-333-7152

04 05 06 07 9 8 7 6 5 4 3 2 1

Printed in the United States of America

ACKNOWLEDGMENTS

The author would like to acknowledge the following for their heartfelt support, unrepentant rejection, or unabashed apathy, all of which have played key roles in giving said author the energy, drive, and material to complete this work. You know who you are, and it is the opinion of this author that you deserve recognition for contributing: First, my family, friends and coworkers, and especially my bandmates, who have stuck by me despite my best efforts to sabotage my entire world at times ... reminding me over and over again through your words and actions that there is hope, and it is found in relationship. Second, every band that created music that mattered along the way, showing me that there is indeed reward for sticking to your guns, and that despite the fact that this industry only kills, you made something that made we want to live, and live on the road. Third, every single supporter and fan who bought an album, a T-shirt, or a book I wrote, even if after buying said materials you realized that I wasn't the spiritual guru some would like to have made me into. Fourth, every single relationship with the opposite sex which ended in utter bloody massacre and tragedy, because without those mistakes I would have no material, and you, failed loves, would never have been immortalized. Fifth, all the former members of our Project 86 team who fell by the wayside or left our side because opportunism was more important than loyalty. Again, you know who are, and I am here to acknowledge you for giving me the nerve to keep going, even though in your actions you tried to prove to me (and my band) that we were nothing special. Forgiveness is real, former friends, for the repentant heart, and I for one believe in it despite my frustration. Finally, the author would like to acknowledge himself for being naive enough to ever make the mistake of thinking that music can heal wounds. This last is less of an acknowledgment and more of a confession deserving no credit whatsoever, other than the fact I couldn't think of anything better to do with the last eight years of my life than pour my mistakes and heartache into our sound.

TABLE OF CONTENTS

IT'S ALL DOWN FROM HE

CHAPTER 1
A REALLY REALLY BAD DREAM

PROJECTS

CHAPTER 1
A REALLY REALLY BAD DREAM

EVERYONE HAS THEM. THERE'S THE ONE ABOUT FALLING from a ten-story window into a wading pool, always ending with opened eyes just before impact. Then there's the one about the unspeakable monster chasing you through the night while you are in your pajamas, and you can't run and you can't scream for help. And then there's the one about your teeth falling out in a bloody mess running down your best suit. And on and on down the line ... the one about the alligator waiting for you in your bedroom when you have to use the bathroom in the middle of the night, the one about your grandmother becoming a vampire, and the one about a little green man just outside your window. Everyone has them.

We often transfer our deepest fears and insecurities into symbolic beasts that manifest themselves through our subconscious minds in our dreams. Most can be easily written off when you awake. Most disappear from memory within moments of the sunlight hitting our open eyes in the morning. But every now and then, there is a nightmare so unspeakable, so terrible, that it sticks with us for weeks, months, even years. These are the unexplainable, unimaginable images that are so real and so believable that they cannot be shrugged away. In my world, the worst, most devastatingly horrible, most incredibly gruesome nightmare on planet earth, is the one about our drummer Alex, the sold out show, and the stuffed animals. That's right—I said, ALEX, A SOLD OUT SHOW, AND STUFFED ANIMALS. Scared? You should be.

We are late to a festival in the Pacific Northwest called Tomfest. We drive through the mountains at what seems like a snail's pace. Then I notice that it seems slow because cars are flying past us at breakneck speed, honking and screaming obscenities as they pass. We are only traveling six miles an hour. I am screaming at the top of my lungs for Alex to speed up, but he cannot hear me. He is eating gigantic sunflower seeds and spitting them onto the floor of our van. And when I say gigantic, I mean they look like they came from a seventeen-foot flower, if that were even possible. The sound of his slurping fills the atmosphere, the air, the space inside my skull like a dog whistle to a canine. He laughs, telling stories and spitting, not seeming to be aware that we are late for our show. I am screaming at the top of my lungs, over and over again, for him to step on it. I have been screaming all the way from home, an eighteen-hour drive all in all from Orange County to Northern Oregon. Alex has drool and spit and seeds all over his body, caked and dried to his skin. And then I notice he isn't wearing any clothing—only tighty-whities. He is actually wearing a sunflower seed outfit, glued to him with dried spit. To someone standing far away, it would just look like a brown sweater with matching brown pants. I mean, he has always annoyed me before with his sunflower seed driving habit, but come on.

I look at Randy, our guitarist, and his mouth is ten times larger than it normally is, with a grin so huge that it stretches over his forehead, his ears, and his chin. His teeth are huge and chipped, with gaps in between them so large that you can see his massive tongue pulsing and twitching behind them. They look like six-inch pieces of rotted ivory. When he laughs, his mouth opens wide enough to fit an entire human head into. His gums are swollen and puffy, purple more than pink, with bloody cuts and bulging veins. In between his massive laughter fits, he turns to me and breathes on my face, sending my hair flailing in the breeze. It smells like barbequed baby turd. I feel a gag coming on. I can't believe it; he has actually become one big mouth, no doubt because his loud voice and constant, wake-the-dead laughter has always shredded my nerves.

Apparently, they are both laughing at me, because they keep looking back at me and pointing. I continue screaming, and as I do, they laugh even harder, shaking the entire van as we drive. I hold on for dear life as I am knocked around the inside of the vehicle, a little confused as to where the earthquake is coming from. Then I figure it out. It's Randy's voice that shakes the van. The cycle continues … scream, fit of insane laughter, scream.

Then there is Steve, our bass player. He is asleep, I think. I can't really tell. He just lays there, silent, in the back of the van. I can't tell if he is sleeping because he has no face. Just flat, smooth skin and ears. And shaggy hair. And sunglasses. He just lays there, as if dead, with headphones on. That's it. No face. Just sleep and headphones and hair and smooth skin. Steve has always been the silent, elusive one, but I guess he has now redefined that title. He turns to look at me, or at least I think he does—how do you really tell if someone with no eyes is looking at you? Then he starts shaking his head at me in disapproval, as if to tell me that I am not helping the situation by screaming. I keep screaming anyway, ignoring Steve's apparent advice as we crawl up the mountains, just a couple of hours away from our destination.

I can't believe it. Every single thing that ever annoyed me about my own band members has become a weapon, and they are using those weapons to try to destroy me.

We inch toward the show, a chorus of earthquakes, smooth skin, blood curdling cries for help, and teeth. Now, this is no ordinary show. It is already sold out, and we are one of the headlining acts, set to perform for more than one hundred and seventy-five thousand people. Granted, these one hundred and seventy-five thousand people will be pretty uncomfortable in a large barn that holds fifteen hundred at the most, which is really the utmost capacity of the venue. I guess the Tomfest promoters did not expect such high ticket revenues, but they oversold the show nonetheless. I am excited and nervous and panicked as usual, but probably even more than normal since my band became deformed monsters very recently, and they all seem to think it is a very funny joke. Joke's on you, Schwab. We are mutants. Surprise!

Anyway, apparently our last minute addition to the festival sold one hundred sixty thousand more tickets for the event. I hear this fact on the radio as we drive, just beneath the slurping, the laughter, and my own screams. The radio DJ continues to talk about our band after mentioning this, and he goes on to say that this is the most anticipated single appearance by a band in the U.S. since The Clash played New York City for seventeen nights in a row back in the '80s. I consider this to be a big reason for us to be on time today, for the first time in our band's history. Our driver, Alex, seems to disagree.

See, prior to his transformation into the sunflower seed death beast, one of Alex's primary functions was to make us late to any and every event possible. This was usually accomplished by adding unnecessary meals, showers, and restroom breaks to an already overly packed schedule, resulting in said lead vocalist wanting to hurt small animals. Yes, I said small animals. And I say small animals because it is impossible to get too angry at Alex for his tardy deeds because he is so freaking lovable. And THIS fact makes me even more insane. I can't stand it when I can't get angry with someone. It makes me want to tear the heads off of, well, chipmunks, small deer, antelope, the occasional baby seal. You get the point. This is all pre-seed mutation, of course. Now I would have no problem dumping hungry dung beetles on him, because he is no longer human. He is just a drummer/monster.

I put my hand to my head to cover my ears, and half of my hair comes out in my hands. I scream again, and my two loving bandmates roar with earthshaking laughter once again. Then Alex looks back at me for what seems like over a minute and just stares, drooling sunflower seed residue and smiling at me. He has several teeth missing. This fact is really not important to me because he has completely taken his eyes off the road ahead of him, turning completely around in his chair.

"WATCH THE ROAD, ALEX!! ARE YOU TRYING TO KILL US?! WHAT'S WRONG WITH YOU?!?!" I exclaim so loud my vocal chords seem to stretch and threaten to explode. Then I realize the sound is only in my head, the words momentarily covering over the sound of Randy's laughter in my brain. They have all finally become the monsters I always knew they were. Randy is one big mouth. Alex is a drooling, tardy, sunflower seed-laden psychopath who will certainly drive us off a cliff. And of course, Steve is just a terrifying faceless scarecrow jamming to his headphones in the back of the van. All of my fears have come true in one fell swoop. Or so I thought. The reality is that this all is just a prelude, an introduction, an opening ceremony. I blink ...

... And the next thing I know, I am at the festival. What? Who?
How? I was just in that van under the control of complete maniacs
who used to be my band members, and now we are here. I blink
again, and when my eyes open, I am still here. I can walk, talk, and
even speak at normal volume. Steve is standing beside me, and he
has a face. A normal face. I see Randy talking to some teenage girls,
and they are not running in terror. He is no longer just a mouth. I
walk up to Steve and ask him where Alex is.

"He went to go make phone call. He should be back soon. We
have to play in like forty-five minutes, so you had better get ready,
Schwab."

There aren't one hundred and seventy-five thousand people here,
but there sure are a lot. The festival looks normal. I am not being
hounded by thousands of adoring people and the press. It doesn't
seem to me that we are either late or extraordinarily anticipated.
I look around the festival grounds and watch things go on as they
should. I walk amid a few of the attendees, and they don't seem
to pay me much attention, beyond a few of them saying, "Hello,
Project 86." This is amazing. It must have all been a nightmare. A
really bad one. Strange, I don't even remember arriving here, and
I certainly don't remember sleeping. But here we are, a mid-level
band, appreciated but not adored. Anticipated by hundreds, but not
worshiped. Fairly well-known, but not famous. And we are no longer
a band of three monsters and one terrified frontman. Everything
seems to be in line.

I decide to focus my attention and thoughts on the show we
are about to play instead of harping on the unexplainable sleep
phenomenon that has just occurred. Some things are better left
unexplained. In fact, it was so amazingly scary that I don't even want
to go there. Gone. Done. Finished thinking about it forever. A shiver

creeps up my spine as I stand there in the cool northwest breeze, gazing at the picturesque mountain backdrop behind the festival grounds.

Minutes pass, and all of a sudden it is time for our band to begin setting up to play. Steve, Randy, and the festival ground crew begin to load the guitar gear onstage and set up. I watch from behind the stage as the crowd of at least eight hundred begins showing hints of excitement for our set. This incites my anticipation for the show, and I begin pacing back forth, back and forth, on edge.

Why am I so nervous? Because Alex is nowhere to be found. We have fifteen minutes to get the all the gear loaded onto stage before we line check, then ten more minutes after that to line check, and then we play. Right now, at this moment, we are dangerously close to running behind schedule. The drum gear is still safely locked in the trailer behind the stage. I begin to simmer. I yell at Steve, then Randy, but they don't even look my way or acknowledge me in any way. So, I decide to break the cardinal pre-show rule and walk onstage before it is time to play (killing the mood, mystique, and glamour of my glorious entrance), hoping that if I confront my other band members, they will be able to tell me where our disappearing little Alex has run off to. A few fans yell my name as I walk up there, my back to the audience.

"Where is Alex?" I ask Steve as he is wiring his bass gear. He responds with a shrug in typical Steve fashion—no stress, no confrontation, no worries. He is content to be concerned with his responsibilities and nothing beyond that. So, I gallop across the stage and get in Randy's face, hoping he gives me the information I need to hear to put my mind at ease. I pose the same question, and he just ignores me. So I ask again.

"Dude, I said, do you know where our drummer is?"

"Schwab, I really need to focus on getting my gear set up. I am sure everything will be fine. Don't stress." He makes a mocking face at me as he says this, which is what Randy excels at. Any time I try to pull things together and be the leader I have been appointed to be, he opposes me with passive-aggressiveness. I would really like to backhand him right now, but I can't in front of the kids.

Oh, and another thing: Don't ever tell me not to stress when there is a definitive something to stress about. In fact, don't ever tell me not to stress, period. Relaxed people have always made me nervous. How am I going to prepare for the imminent disaster that is always waiting for me if I don't worry about it first? That whole reverse-psychology thing works in both directions, to be certain. Yup, the most surefire way to make me into the severely fragile, anal replica of myself is to make me aware of my own anxiety problem. It's like calling critical attention to any physical aspect of a female in conversation. Bad policy, always, without exception. It will always come back to bite you in some way. Besides, it is my responsibility to make sure this whole thing runs smoothly, and if I don't take it upon myself to make things happen, no one else will. I didn't ask for the role. It's just that right now it seems like I am the only one who even cares whether or not this show happens. I can feel my temples beginning to pulse with the pressure that is being exerted throughout my body. And still no drummer. I zip across the stage again, avoiding eye contact with the audience, primarily because the expression on my face, as I am well aware, closely resembles the face I would be making had I been forced to swallow someone else's earwax.

As I drop back down to the floor and make my way behind the stage and outside again, the heavens part, the stars align, and my prayers are answered. Heaven has once again heard my cries and has delivered to me my drummer. I begin to run toward him with complete joy and relief, but my feet stop moving when I notice his clothing.

He is walking out of the bathroom wearing running shorts, a clean white T-shirt, and house slippers. He has a bath towel draped over his shoulder, as he has just gotten out of the shower. To make matters much, much worse, he is now talking on his cell phone, pacing back and forth like that gorilla on *Donkey Kong*. Alex is the guy who will be buried with his cell phone, and he is the ultimate phone-pacer, which also adds to his long list of Schwab-stressing attributes. (At this point, I have to let you in on a video game idea that myself and my other band members have concocted in honor of Mr. Alex Albert, our fine percussionist. It will be called Mad Cell Phone Wanderer, and it is a shooting game that involves—you guessed it—plucking off as many wandering cell phone toters as possible. It's actually not that much different from games like *Grand Theft Auto* and whatever other shooting games are hot with the kiddies today, except the cell phone wanderers don't shoot back at you. They just pace so fast across the screen that they are nearly impossible to get a bead on. I imagine there will be many different levels, one involving a mall scene, another with a gas station scene, etc. The final level of the game involves destroying Verizon Headquarters with an atomic bomb. Now, don't steal our idea; the franchise rights alone will make us rich beyond our wildest dreams.) I draw closer to Alex, the excitement clearly gone from my face, and yes, I once again look like I have eaten something vile. I can hear Alex's conversation, which he is having with his girlfriend of six years, Becca.

"But, Baybee, I really miss you, and you know I will be home very soon. Let's not do this now. Please. Please? I know. I know. I know! Really?! I love you, too. Yeah, I will make sure we get home as fast as possible and—hold on, Pookoo, I have a call on the other line. Hello?

Hey, man! What's happening? Doing great! How are you? Nothing much, nothing much. We are just up in the Northwest playing a show. That's cool! Tell your wife I said hello! H-h-hold on man, I am on the other line—yeah? Oh, man!! That's so cool! Totally! I will be there! We will be home in a couple days. H-h-hold on a second, K? Cool. Babe? Yeah, hey, can I call you back in five minutes? I know, I'm sorry. Five minutes? Okay. Love you, too. K, man, I am all yours."

As you can imagine, this continues for what seems like 137,546 hours, and by this point, I am seriously ready to take his cell phone out of his hand, stomp on it like Jim Carrey, then hand it back to him in bits. Instead, I close the distance between us and tap him on the shoulder. He responds by putting his finger up and avoiding eye contact with me. He continues with his conversation. I tap him again. And again. And again.

"What, dude?!" he says to me, very offended that I have interrupted this small talk convention that he is hosting with long-lost relatives before the most important show of our lives.

"Sorry to put you out, but we have a show to do, and we need your drum gear onstage immediately. We are already in danger of cutting into our set if you don't get set up in the next five minutes. Get off the phone and load your gear onstage." I say this calmly and coldly, in my best DMV employee tone, to drive the point home that the situation is getting desperate.

"Dude, chill, can't you see I am on the phone? Give me two minutes, and I will be there. Go check on Steve and Randy and make sure they are getting set up. I will be there in two minutes, I promise. Don't stress, Schwab." I shake my head, look to the ground, and turn to leave. Behind me I hear the meaningless trivia convo commence once again. I return to the side of the stage, and now I am pacing again in plain sight of the audience. As it turns out, this is only the beginning.

Minutes pass, but it's more like moons. I pace impotently behind the stage, waiting, hoping. It is twelve minutes before we are scheduled to play. No sign of Alex or his drum kit. No sign of peace for me either, at least anytime soon. Steve and Randy have finished setting their gear up and are standing up onstage, strumming away without a care in the world. Funny how that works. *Let Schwab handle it*, they think to themselves. *We'll just stand here and strum, and let him stress.* They don't even make eye contact with me. I am now talking to myself, out loud, as I continue to pace behind the stage.

"Why am I the only one who cares ... why am I the only who cares ... why am I the only one who cares ... why am I—" My words are cut off by, bless the Maker, an approaching Alex, this time dressed and ready for the show. And not a moment too soon. We are due onstage in five minutes, and the crowd is beginning to chant our name. PRO-JECT. PRO-JECT. PRO-JECT. PRO-JECT. I can see kids floating on top of the crowd from my vantage point, turning, careening off of one another as the sea of bodies begins to come to a boil. This is amazing. I have never seen such anticipation at a show, let alone one of our shows. I can feel the walls shaking as the kids pound in unison, rhythmically with their chants. A smile creeps over my sullen face. It is all going to work out, as it always does. What was I so worried about? Alex is late, sure, as expected. And maybe we will have to cut into our set for a song or two while he sets up. No big deal. This is going to be the best show of our lives. I can feel the energy of that room pulsing through my skin, piercing through to my heart. I wouldn't want to be anywhere else in the known universe than here, now. That is, of course, until I look back at Alex as he approaches.

He is holding a giant box in his hands, the size of his kick drum to be exact, as he bounces toward the stage with a huge, Gomer Pyle grin on his face. *This is all fine*, I think. *Apparently he has come into a new drum kit in the last ten minutes. That explains the box.* But as he gets closer, I see that it is no kick drum box. The lid is open, and there is something small and fuzzy poking out of the top. I look closer, but can't make out what it is, so I run up to him just before he makes it to the back edge of the stage.

"Whatcha got in your box, there, Alex?" I say in my best gentle voice, so as not to spook him, hoping that my tone will soothe him into setting up his drums.

"Dude, chill, it's under control." The look on his face is blank. He stares not into my eyes, but through them, with a huge, dumb grin pasted to his skull. He has the look of child who has just successfully completed his first big-boy number one on the adult commode. Then it happens. I reach to my tip-toes and peer over the edge of the box. My eyes must be deceiving me. I rub them and look again. Inside the box is a huge pile of charred stuffed animals and assorted trash. Gum wrappers, McDonald's Happy Meal boxes, and ripped pillows. But mostly it is just old stuffed animals that have been discarded after some sort of fire destroyed them. It is at this point that I feel my fragile grip on my sanity give way.

"Alex, what in the world are you doing?!"

"Out of my way, dude." He rips the box of out my hands, jumps up to the stage, and dumps the contents of the entire box all over the place. It fills the entire platform with a small layer of junk. I can now see that all the stuffed animals were once mine. There are several imitation Cabbage Patch Kids, which brings back a distant memory of my eighth birthday. My grandmother made them for me, thinking that I would enjoy them. I remember trying to muster up the strength to act grateful for them, when all I really wanted was Atari 2600 Games. They ended up at the back of my closet, hidden and buried not two weeks later so as to avoid any future embarrassment when my friends came in my room. I even remember the names she gave them on the tags she created and sewed on them. Jake Ryan, Joshua Ralph, and Greg Sully. There is also a load of assorted bears, frogs, Disney characters, and bunnies. Lots of bunnies. And they all have been burned and covered in ketchup. At least I think it is ketchup. The alternative reality I do not even want to consider ... as in, "Where (or who) did all that blood come from?" Here, in a nutshell, is a quarter of my childhood toys, all of which I was ashamed of. All of them given as gifts from the day I was born to age nine by relatives who had somehow forgotten the fact that I was a MALE child. I remember Freddy the Froggy, as my aunt so affectionately named him. Freddy's left eye has now been ripped out, replaced with a smudge of ketchup. His good eye stares at me from the floor of the stage, our stage, as Alex leaps and bounds joyously around, kicking and throwing everything so as to make sure it is evenly distributed. I stand, unable to move. Then, he grabs his box, jumps down to the ground, and takes off running. He has disappeared again. I don't even try to grab him as he passes me. I can't. I have no strength left. I am completely and utterly dumbfounded.

I turn and look at the crowd, then to Steve, then to Randy, then back to the crowd again. Steve and Randy are laughing. They're laughing! And as they laugh, they continue to strum chords, warming up, it seems, for the show that is nowhere nearer to happening as it was a half an hour ago. Then I realize they are not warming up. They are creating a soundtrack for the moment, egging Alex on with out-of-tune notes. Funny, they have been standing up there for fifteen minutes tuning their instruments, and they aren't even in tune. The sounds coming from their amps are horrible, sour, bitter.

Now, the crowd has stopped its chants and cheers. They stare at the stage as confused as I am. The place is completely silent, except, of course, for the improv jam session that my two band members are conducting. Everyone is looking at one another, perhaps searching for an answer, but none can be found. I can see eyes searching for me, praying that I can somehow take control of the situation. We are now ten minutes late for our performance. If Alex does not set up soon, we will only be able to play a couple of songs before we are cut off.

Have you ever felt like the world is out to get you? Have you ever, as you walk throughout your day, felt the sensation that people are watching you, eyeing you, plotting against you with whispers of your secret sins, your skeletons, your weaknesses? Have you ever walked through the mall thinking that someone is following you, waiting for you to exit and get into your car so they can follow you home and grab you just before you walk in the door? That is this feeling that follows me everywhere I walk. I have had it since I was very young. It is a voice that says, "They are out to get you, Schwab. They are just waiting for the opportune moment so they can leap from the shadows and spring upon you." I never know when the conspiracy will manifest itself, but it is there, lurking and growing among the people who I am supposed to trust the most. Why do I feel this way? I have no idea. Call it intuition. Call it isolation or paranoia or whatever you want to call it. All I know is that at almost every hour of every day, I feel this lurking, dormant fear. And at this very hour, it has all come true. My band members have finally chosen the right moment to spring, unleashing the fury of all my fears upon me on what is supposed to be the greatest day of my waking life.

Steve and Randy continue to giggle and play, not making eye

contact with me. The audience is now starting to grab a few of the animals and bat them around like beach balls. Randy and Steve are infecting them with their "music." I hear the faint rumble of laughter as it speeds through the audience like a seismic wave. Okay. Must collect what is left of myself. Must collect sanity at all costs. Must save show. Must find Alex and beat some sense into him.

I close my eyes and breathe. I now have a mission, and that is to save this freaking show or die trying. I open my eyes again and sprint to our van, hoping to find my drummer. He is not around or in it. I then begin roaming the festival grounds in an agonized race against time, praying that I find him. And when I do, I will drag him to the stage, kicking and screaming. I pull my cell phone from my pocket and try to dial his number. Funny how I didn't think of this before. If there is one thing that can be counted on in this life, it is that Alex will have his cell phone with him, charged and ready. It is his life's blood. I dial. It rings ... and rings. But just as I am about to hang, up he answers.

"Hello?"

"ALEX! WHERE ARE YOU? WE HAVE TO GET ON AND PLAY NOW! PLEASE, BY ALL THAT IS RIGHT AND HOLY, GET TO THE STAGE AND GET READY TO PLAY. THERE IS STILL TIME!!"

"Dude, can I call you back? I am on the other line with my woman. H-h-hold on, I will call you right back, dude. Two minutes, I promise." Click.

"ALEX! ALEX!?" I fall to the earth, world in a haze. Defeat has found me. They have beaten me. I have failed. I lay on my back as blackness descends. The angel of death has found me for sure. And it has the face of my drummer, grinning madly and talking on his cell phone.

My eyes open. Where … oh, no! Have to get up and save the show! I must have fallen asleep. I jump up and race for the stage. I can see the barn, just a few hundred feet away, and I can hear the crowd roaring! We are going to play! I can hear them. Alex must have heard my cries. He must have felt my pain! Yes! YES!! My feet accelerate and carry me around to the back of the barn, where I will, no doubt, find my band standing, prepared to go on. Now I see, now I understand! This was all a joke, a bad, bad joke, to make me loosen up for the show. The guys knew I would be intense today, so they just played a little hoax on me to help me to relax. I get it now. It's all so clear as day, and now I am ready, so ready, to perform. Just a few more yards and I will be there. Just a few more steps and I will round the corner of the building to my waiting band members. There's the corner. I turn it …

… And stop in my tracks. I almost collide with Alex as he is sprinting to the stage from the opposite direction. He is carrying that box again, this time overflowing with, no … no way. I refuse to believe it. MORE STUFFED ANIMALS. No. I lose it, completely. I throw myself at him to tackle him, and he throws a mean stiff arm at me, spins, and bounces toward the stage again, whistling. I land in a puddle of mud, rocks, and earthworms, scraping my face in the process. I think I broke my jaw. From the mud, I roll over in agony and try to see what is going on.

I can see it all plainly. There is no drum kit set up, and the festival crew is beginning to tear down our guitar gear. Then I see what the crowd was roaring about; Alex has been a busy man in my absence. I was only gone for a few minutes, but he has effectively covered the ENTIRE stage now with a layer three feet deep of trash. He is kicking it around and frolicking madly. The crowd is roaring because they are watching Alex completely lose his mind right in front of them.

And I don't hear even a hint of disappointment in that roar. They are entertained, much more so, even, than if we had played and put on the show of our lives. I truly am, now, the only person on the face of the planet who cares that this, the most important of shows, has been devoured by a madman's twisted dance recital in huge pile of crap.

I twist my aching frame over and raise myself to my knees so I can see the entire morbid scene clearly. Alex kicks and stomps and dances and twists wildly as Steve and Randy watch from the side of the stage, wailing in delight. His dance is almost Irish. He raises his left hand and knee in unison, then does the same with the opposing side. I don't find it the least bit entertaining. I just kneel in my puddle of worms, wondering what has become of my band and my friends. They have turned on me, and I can only watch. I see Freddy the Froggy dangling from the rafters, dripping ketchup onto the heads in the first row. Freddy, which was once my plaything, is now a mangled ornament. Now he is a part of my demise, hanging on for dear life from those metal beams, his one eye staring at me with a look of S.O.S. Maybe it is not too late. Maybe, just maybe, there is time for one final gasp of energy to make this thing happen.

I draw myself to my feet and leap forward, bumping into a few kids who are exiting the stage area. Mud drips from my eyebrows, my shoelaces, and everything in between. I am a vision that belongs at Woodstock in the trenches with the pitters. As I push through these kids, one of them turns and points at me with an astonished look on his face.

"Is that Andrew?" he asks one of his friends.

"Yeah, I think so, and he looks mad!" the friend answers.

"HEY, ANDREW, DON'T WORRY ABOUT IT, MAN! I THINK THIS IS THE BEST SHOW I HAVE EVER SEEN!" the kid yells.

They all share in laughter. Boy, everyone here seems to be quite cheery. I look back over my shoulder briefly and give the two kids a disgusted glare, just before I turn to put Alex out of commission once and for all. That's it! If I can't play a show today, my only mission is to destroy the very person who has foiled me on this day. I see my target in my sights, covered in ketchup with McDonald's wrappers sticking to various points on his body. He shows no signs of slowing or abating, and seems to be continuing to gain strength from the jaunts of the mass before him. Behind him the band that is to play after us is now setting up amid his revelry. Our gear is now gone, nowhere to be found. Steve and Randy are now in the front row of the crowd, joining in the fun. Even the crew of the festival clap and smile as they watch Alex's display of dance moves. As I stealthily approach the side, he changes his dance, this time to some hip-hop/running man move.

That's it. Enough! I have to find a way to end this, and NOW. Irish folk dances without music is one thing, but the pain of watching hip-hop dancing without music by the most uncoordinated and unrhythmic drummer ever created is quite another. This is the final straw, kids.

I lunge through the security on the side of the stage as they attempt to hold me back. But I claw, bite, scream, and kick my way through the wall of meatheads and find myself alone, on the stage with Alex. In a matter of microseconds, I am on his back, bringing him to his knees in a huge mound of crap. I wrap my legs around his waist from behind, my hands seizing his ears and twisting as he buckles beneath me.

"YOU ARE CRAZY, MAN! DO YOU REALIZE WHAT YOU HAVE DONE?" I scream into his ears as he fights for air beneath me in the toys and trash. He is saying something back to me from below, but I can't hear him through the crowd noise, which has turned from excited cheers to boos and threats. Evidently the audience does not share in my appraisal of the situation. No matter. This all has to end because reason must return to reign in my world, and no crazy band members are going to keep me from reclaiming that cherished sanity.

Suddenly, I am seized from behind and put into a full nelson. The audience cheers even louder! I am being leveraged away from Alex, but I am still holding his ears in my hands, twisting harder and harder. If I am pulled away, I am going to take his ears with me.

"GET OFFFFFF! GET OFFFFFFF!" I scream, over and over again. Then I feel an intense sting in the side of my neck, as if someone is trying to filet the skin right next to my jugular. I am being bitten by the pro wrestler who slapped this sleeper hold on me. I instantly let go of my grip on Alex's ears as teeth sink into my neck, drawing blood for sure.

"AAAAAAH!" I shriek into the dank concert air. This is what they all came for, right? To hear me scream? My cries of pain draw new excitement from the onlookers. The roar of the painfully delighted crowd shakes the ground beneath us, as my (former) drummer breaks free, tossing his pile of junk into the air like a million dollar winner on a game show, over and over again. He doesn't even look back at me as I am being lifted and hauled away, still held in a full nelson by the linebacker/security guard who is carrying me. My look of terror is focused on him as I reach toward him while being pulled away in the opposite direction. The last thing I see before the world goes black again is him, with his two index fingers pointed in the air from extended arms. He has raised his hands to the heavens to proclaim ultimate victory over me in front of the sold out crowd.

My eyes open. I am in the van again. There are no stuffed animals, no trash, no dancing drummers. I lay in the back bed, awake from a nap. I look forward to the driver's seat and see Alex, alert as usual, with a huge bag of Jalapeno sunflower seeds in his lap (with, of course, his handy-dandy empty cup next to him on the console). Randy sits shotgun, reading a magazine and laughing every seven seconds or so. Steve is not with us, because ... because? ... oh, I remember. It's because he is flying out to the show to meet us because he has to go to a wedding. I have this feeling of waning dread in my stomach, recalling vivid, yet scattered visions of old toys, ketchup, and laughter. It's hazy, but I know I have just awoken from a pretty intense nightmare. I am a little sweaty, probably more from the faulty air conditioning in the van than terror. Nonetheless, at this moment, it is a beautiful thing to be outside the confines of the images that were playing in my mind's eye not more than moments ago. We are on our way to Ohio to play a show. Now I remember it all, as the dream world fades into oblivion. We are somewhere in the desert not far from home, having left only a few hours before. It is all fading into a comfortable place, but I know that I have just experienced some monumental trauma inside myself.

And for the next few hours, I know Alex and his sunflower seeds will grate more than ever on my nerves, though I am not sure exactly why. I look outside to the desert and can see a vague silhouette on the side of the road as we pass. At first it looks like a huge, white stuffed bunny, but then I realize it is a cop car slumbering quietly on the side of the road.

CHAPTER 2
A LASER POINTER AND A HOSTAGE SITUATION

CHAPTER 2
A LASER POINTER AND A HOSTAGE SITUATION

I AM IMMORTAL.

I am invincible.

I am freedom.

Freedom. It is a fragile thing, really. It is a thing so earnestly sought after, yet it is so elusive. Say it to yourself: Freeeeedom. Everyone wants it. Everyone spends most of their waking lives fighting for it, scraping and clawing with rush hour traffic, retirement plans, and forty-hour weeks. We fight for it because we know once we have it, we will be owned by no one. Not The Man, not his minions. It is the absence of care, of burden, and in my mind, responsibility.

And today it is mine.

My own freedom on my own terms. For me, this very idea is captured in one simple word: TOUR. Today we leave. Today we are our own. Today we embark on journeys unknown. Today is the first day of our very first national tour as a band, and I am ecstatic, proud, impatient. Today we make our own rules with our instruments, our voices on the long highway. Today we belong to no one but ourselves.

Today we wave goodbye to the bosses and nine to fives and dull daily ritual of orthodoxy. We are our own. We belong to no one.

We are Project 86. We are unstoppable. We own our destinies.

It is sometime in the fall of 1998. We have been a band for two years, but now we have a record deal with an independent label, and our first album is coming out next month, so it is time to hit the road. We have a show in forty-eight hours in the state of Ohio, some twenty-seven hundred miles away from our safe suburban homes in sunny Orange County, California. It is the first show of a mini tour we are doing over the next two weeks, and we have decided that instead of spending money on hotel rooms, we will drive those two days straight, only stopping for gas and food. Under normal circumstances, this would be a daunting task for four members of an ordinary band. But then, we are no ordinary band.

We are Project 86.

We are super humans fueled by the dream, the love: full-time misiciandom. And at this point in our young career, we would sacrifice anything for the cause.

Anything for the dream, the love. We are Project 86.

Unstoppable. Invincible. Immortal. Free.

Now, before I tell you my little story, let's talk for a moment, kids, about the first day of tour, which is today. I know, I know. Setups are boring, but they must be done. Even Tom Clancy takes fifty pages or so to set up his stories, so you can bear with me for a few measly paragraphs here. I promise it gets better. Anyways, the first day of tour is the most dreadful day of the whole year when you are in a rock band. At least in *our* rock band. I mean, it is the *worst*. Everything seems to take 197 hours longer than it is supposed to. The only thing you want to do is get on the road. You have made all your preparations for days; you are mentally motivated and beyond excited to be on that lonely road between here and the next show, far away from all responsibility and care.

And yet, like that beautiful orange carrot that dangles just microns away from your outstretched fingertips, *the road* is the only thing you can't quite seem to have. You have paid all your bills, kissed your mother on the forehead (while she secretly despises your career choice, despite the fact that you are a college graduate and will most certainly become a college professor some day—to her delight—when your rock 'n' roll fantasies have run their course. Ah, who can blame her? Mother knows best), and left your soon-to-be-ex girlfriend a box of Sees Candies (soon-to-be-ex because they always find someone else when you leave for tour). Good-bye. So long, mundane life, at least for a couple of weeks. I have more important and more exciting things ahead of me, things that will make me the envy of my peers, the hero of my old neighborhood … except that very thing is now, at this moment, no closer to me that it was months ago, because this day will never end. We will NEVER get on the road—at least no time in the near future.

We will never leave, it seems, because the day we leave for tour is the longest day ever created.

I arrive at Alex's house on time, 7 a.m. on the dot, and he is still in bed. I pound on the back door of his mother's house while his painfully ecstatic dog, Valentine, wipes its muddy mitts all over the back of my khaki Dickies (have you ever noticed that khaki Dickies ALWAYS get dirty within three hours of purchase?). His mother comes to the door and screams "Valentine!" between her teeth, which are clenched the way every member of Alex's family has concluded will shut this freaking dog's yap. Alex does the same thing every time I come to his house. As the dog shrieks in delight (or is it pain?) at incoming visitors, he screams the animal's name between his clenched teeth so the sound comes out muffled. Think Jonathan Davis from Korn. *And it works.* In fact, it is the only thing that works to quiet the thing. So, at this moment, I am a member of the Albert family, yelling "Valentine!" over and over again between my clenched teeth. The dog cowers and returns to its doghouse. Did I mention Alex is still asleep? We have fifty-three hours and counting to make our trip. And where is Randy? He should be here by now. Impatient, I call Randy's house. His dad answers and puts him on the phone.

"Hhheelloooh," he says, his voice groggy. I can tell he is still sleeping. A thought goes through my head to threaten him with some form of physical abuse if I do not see his face in five minutes (funny—because he lives twenty minutes away).

"Are you packed yet, at least?" I mutter into the phone. He just giggles and hangs up on me.

I don't call Steve, our bass player, because he will not be joining us on our trip to Ohio. He has a wedding to attend at home and will be flying out to meet us. Yes, that's right, we only have three drivers for our endless journey. I breathe deeply and shut my eyes.

So, here I sit, alone on Alex's front step, seething with impotent anticipation.

Since I have some time to kill, I decide to go to the coffee shop up the street to find some food in the hope that it will relieve the impatience that is already building in me. We haven't even left yet, and already my nerves are being stretched. I look back as Alex's mom walks into the house to awake her slumbering son. This is what I go through, not yet two years into this band (we have played many shows on the West Coast, but never anywhere else). We have never done a full national tour, and this day must be perfect. I won't have it any other way.

I could have slept in a lot longer. I skipped breakfast to get here on time. We have a million miles to go and thirty seconds to get there. And these guys can't even set an alarm? Does my complaint sound reasonable, or do my words sound reminiscent of a fascist dictator? All I know is that this is going to be a long, long day. True words, indeed. Only, I have no idea how true they will prove to be at this point. I go, grab some food, and return with my best happy face on, to greet my band members, who are finally awake and ready, one hour later. Better late than dead, I guess.

Six hours and endless packing and unpacking of band gear (because we can't seem to get everything to fit into our rented, rickety, U-haul trailer), merchandise (our first T-shirts ever, featuring a large picture of yours truly on the back), and needless entertainment accessories (like a Playstation 1, which will drive us nuts because Alex will obsessively play it all hours of the day and night) later, our van is packed and ready for war. It sags in the rear like a granny in the winter of her life. We got her with a few miles already on her, one hundred thousand to be exact. She is maroon and sleek and as long as can be. She once towed senior citizens back and forth from a nearby retirement community and the mall. Now she is the glutton for our punishment with five thousand pounds or so strapped to her back end in our trailer. What was once a blank, vast interior just hours ago is now riddled with endless pillows, blankets, CD booklets, Playstation accessories, and a television mounted to the base of an old milk crate between the two front seats. Despite the clutter, it is organized and tidy. This will all change soon enough, along with the aroma. It is amazing what horrid smells three or four young men can produce in a sweaty journey through the varying climates of America. I believe the acronym is "F-A-N." I will leave it up to you to decipher what these three awful letters stand for. Suffice it to say that the touring vehicle of a rock band is neither for the faint of heart nor stomach.

At last, we are ready to depart. At least, this is my thought at 3 p.m. on this fine fall afternoon. But I am wrong, of course. One band member (who shall remain nameless, but I will give you a hint: he plays a rhythm instrument that isn't a bass) always seems to need to do two things when time is of the essence: Pee and eat. Pee and eat. Pee and eat. If you would have told me ages ago that a majority of my touring hours for seven years-plus of my life would be spent at the mercy of these two bodily desires of one particular drumming band member, I would have laughed and called you insane. But here we are, eons away from leaving because our drummer has to eat before leaving. And when I say eat, I don't mean Carl's Jr. or Del Taco. Oh noooo. He must have a sit-down meal, or he will not feel complete before he leaves home. We go to the nice Mexican place up the street from his mom's house for our going away meal. There is no room for debate on this issue (because when Alex wants something, he must have it, and debating him on it is more trouble than just giving him what he wants. Yes, I know. This is not unlike how parents deal with screaming toddlers), though Randy and I are absolutely bursting at the seams to get the you-know-what out of Dodge.

And so we eat. And it is good eats. But man-oh-man-oh-man does it come with a price. Mexican food and three boys in a small space. Do you need me to do the math? I am full; I am fattened. And I ask Alex if there is anything else under heaven that needs to be done before we can fly, fly away.

"Only one little thing," he says. "Gas."

Oh no. Anything but that, Lord. Please. Tell me he is joking. I specifically remember reminding him to do that last night.

"Are you serious?" I ask.

"C'mon dude, don't be so antsy. I couldn't get gas last night. I had to take my girlfriend's brother's dog to the vet because her grandmother's sister was out of town. It's cool, man. Chill." Little note: Alex's busy schedule is constantly cluttered with endless errands for members of his girlfriend's family. Don't ask.

Another note: Alex and I turn each other's nerves into shredded Sloppy Joe the second we get in the van. I could go a little easier on the guy in these pages, but then you wouldn't be as entertained by this one-sided, passive-aggressive book written to specifically get back at my band for all the headaches they have caused. Off to the gas station we go.

Now, an interesting enigma on the road is the gas stop phenomenon: home of the dreaded "trinkets." Before you ask, "trinkets" are any type of snack, be it beef jerky, Lorna Doone's shortbread cookies, or Tostitos Scoops (which are incomplete without heated cheese dip, might I add). "Trinkets" will eat your per diem (a per diem is a daily allowance of money for any type of spending you wish—our band makes it on fifteen dollars per day, but I have heard of bands doing as much as thirty, depending on how big the band is and how much income they have coming in) slowly and methodically, without remorse, and replace your hard-earned pay with a gut the size of the great state of Texas.

But this is not all. The dreaded gas stop is also the home of many a wasted moment, where each member does who-knows-what for a minimum of half an hour. Each gas station across the nation has the EXACT same selection of trinkets and pointless souvenirs, too. Yet, after hours and hours locked in a smelly van, even the most routine of stops can seem compelling. I will explain further in later chapters, but suffice it to say that when the band is in a hurry and MUST count every moment as sacred, the dreaded gas stop is an enemy not to be underestimated.

Above all other gas stops is the double-dreaded, monstrosity of all monstrosities, the beast from the pit of hell itself—oh yes, kids, it is the first gas stop BEFORE you actually leave for tour. This is the stop where everyone decides to stock up on everything they forgot to pack, and each band member disappears for at least an hour across the parking lot into the Ralph's grocery store. And Project 86's "before tour" stop is a Mobil station on the corner of Alton Parkway and West Yale Loop in Irvine, California. I can't tell you how much the feeling of dread overcomes me when I see that stupid Mobil station.

So we stop, and sure enough, Alex forgot to bring his wallet. So we turn around, go back to his house, and he decides he needs to call his girlfriend one more time before we leave. Now I sit, again, on his front step, watching him pace on his cell phone up and down the street like a wind-up penguin because he doesn't want to drive until he talks to her one last time. Awesome. He finishes twenty minutes later, and I get to see the Mobil station coming at me all over again as we turn down the road.

The dreaded gas stop lives up to its title. I won't go into to it because it is really pointless. We waste over an hour, and I am turning into a really ugly person. Randy, Alex, and I finally embark on our journey, stocked and amped on Red Bull, Jalapeno sunflower seeds, and low-grade Vanilla Espresso. It is now 5 p.m. That's right. I said FIVE PEEE EMMM. At this point, I am the guy as far as possible from my other band members, sulking on the bed that lies about twelve feet behind the driver's seat.

It is at this point that Randy realizes that he forgot his guitar at home. I bang my head on the window of the van, over and over again. He leaves. I simmer. He returns. I scold him. We drive.

FINALLY.

We come to the third intersection of our drive, barely a quarter mile from Alex's, and suddenly I feel the vehicle jerk with a harsh brake pedal stomp as Alex screams at a driver who nearly broadsides us. Alex screams at the would-be assailant, cursing the other driver's birth at the top of his lungs. Never mind the fact that it is not the other guy who ran the red light, endangering the life of the innocent prima donna vocalist lying on the bed, seatbeltless in the back.

I put my headphones on, allowing my anger to simmer to the tunes of Strife and Snapcase. My fellow bandmates have aptly coined a label for these moments of irritability. They call it "sleep-mode Schwab," because if I fall more than two hours short of my allotted eight hours, you just don't want to even be within shooting distance of my forked tongue. Stay away. FAR away. And today I am the Creatine Monohydrated version of "sleep mode" because I feel cheated and robbed of the shuteye I could have easily grabbed hold of, had I known we would be sitting in Irvine for and extra TEN HOURS. How did we manage to waste ten hours, you ask? Easily. Tack on an extra four for showers and extra sleep for the drummer and the guitarist. Wait two more for the drummer's "mama" to finishing baking us cookies. Then forget necessities like, oh, say, your GUITAR back at home, for which you have to drive half an hour each way to retrieve. Finally, as made so abundantly clear earlier, tack on the dreaded gas stop. Yet, despite my best efforts to remain irate, I cannot help but feel the exhilaration of tour blowing my cares away like rain clouds pushed aside by the fireball in the sky. We are on our way. I am home. The calming hum of our maroon chariot pulses through me, carrying me into a soothing nap before the real fun begins.

Okay, I am now finished setting this thing up so now you, the yawning reader, can begin getting into the real meat of this masterpiece. See, you made it. I told you it wouldn't be that bad.

The sun is down. I awake a short time later and peer out the window with groggy eyes and witness the desert stretching in the darkness to an unseen horizon. We are somewhere on Highway 40, past Barstow, yet still not near the Nevada Border. This is it. I have awoken to heaven from a hazy dream, which is already vanishing from memory. I am on the road. I have caught the forbidden carrot, and endless adventure awaits us. I open the rear window, just to take in the desert air. What will happen on our journey? Who will we meet? What will be the first unforgettable story created? I can hardly contain myself.

I rub my eyes, bring them into focus, and jump to the front seat to sit shotgun next to our driving machine, the great Alex Albert (little note: Alex INSISTS on driving whenever he is conscious because he cannot stand to feel out of control of the vehicle, mostly due to an acute fear involving death while sleeping in a moving van. And, yes—I am a lazy one. I would rather sit in the back of the van and pinpoint the world's weaknesses than partake in meaningless pragmatic activities. Oh yeah, and Alex MUST have sunflower seeds when he drives. And he MUST spit and slurp them at maximum volume, to the dismay of one lead vocalist. Not to mention the fact that said sunflower seeds will eventually and most assuredly end up spilled over the entire floor of the van in an "honest accident" by said drummer, followed by a scream of "I knew it" by a certain someone who sings for Project 86. (I know you already knew all this, but I just wanted to emphasize it).

We have apparently been driving for a few hours, just long enough for everyone to begin forgetting home and start adjusting to the endless concrete that lies ahead.

Now, at this point, Randy begins to get a little restless, which is his

M.O. He can barely focus his attention long enough to write a song, let alone sit calmly and quietly during hours of driving. He is jiggling his knee up and down as he sits in the back seat, searching earnestly for the next short-term form of entertainment. He begins by playing Alex's drumsticks on his knees to the beat of the Sepultura song playing on our desperately weak stereo (we don't have a CD player in the van, and all the speakers are blown). Then he starts clicking the ashtrays open and shut. Cuh-click. Cuh-click. Cuh-click. I feel sleep mode creeping up on me again.

Then, he produces his keys from his pocket. On his key ring is a laser pointer. Why he has this, I have no idea, but it fits Randy nonetheless; he is the king of needless electronic gadgets. He has like fourteen cameras, every video game system, and hundreds of other gadgets I have no idea how he pays for.

Did I mention that laser pointers are also used as sighting systems on several different calibers of high-powered firearms? This is a key detail to remember, friends. Keep that tucked away in the back of your heads. However, this fact seems to elude our giggly, childlike guitar guy (although "guy" is a stretch; he is barely eighteen years old at this point in time). I glance out my window and see a tiny red speck of light bouncing off of road signs and passing trucks like that stupid ping-pong ball over sing-song lyrics on *Sesame Street*—you know, like when Big Bird leads the home audience in the sing-along of "Mary Had a Little Lamb" as Grover plays Mary, bonnet and all.

Now, I know what you are thinking. Andrew, you are the sensible one. Andrew, you the eldest and the most forward thinking. Andrew, you know better. Andrew, though you are incredibly cranky and impatient, you seem to possess some sense. And you are asking me, "Why in the world would you not stop Randy from pointing this thing out the window when other drivers can see it?" And you know, in retrospect, I completely agree with your thought process. But see, somewhere between the excitement of tour and the imminent boredom and dull calm that is the endless highway rests a very thin line. And when you cross that thin line, which separates anticipation from boredom (which takes all of two hours, max), the tiniest of activities, no matter how risky or silly, can provide that much-needed entertainment to get you through. The next thing I know, Alex and I are giving Randy shouts of encouragement on which sign or vehicle to hit with our pretend laser weapon. Yup. We are adult males playing with imaginary blasters. And making the sounds we made at age six, too.

"Hit this truck coming up behind us, Randy. He looks like a potential enemy. He must be destroyed!" we scream with glee. Yes, we are really doing this. This charade continues for all of fifteen minutes, and we are momentarily pacified in the midst our childhood fantasy (much in the microcosmic symbolism of the average rock 'n' roll career—most careers, when boiled down, are a very temporary fulfillment of fantasy, ending when you realize it never was more than a figment of your imagination). What is truly interesting, however, is what diverts our attention from our little game.

Up ahead in the distance, I see the vague form of a vehicle, in seeming hibernation on the median of the freeway. As we approach, we notice it is a police car, no doubt laying a speed trap for unsuspecting truckers. I glance over to the speedometer as we pass. Sixty-eight. We are clean. We laugh to ourselves, knowing that cop will most assuredly be nabbing some other poor sap very soon. But not these poor saps. Oh nooo. Not this night. This night belongs to us. On this very night, we are kings of the planet, immovable, immortal, invincible.

Invincible.

In the midst of our revelry, an odd thing occurs to me, however: We are in the middle of nowhere. What is this cop doing all the way out here? I dismiss the question as soon as it comes and tell Randy to resume with the laser game. Before he has the chance to continue, we notice a second cruiser, this time sitting on the right shoulder of the road. I shoot a look into the side view mirror and watch his lights pop on seconds after we pass. There are several other cars near us on the road, so surely he must be after one of them. I'll bet ten to one that one of these cars has illegal aliens making for the desert in the night. That has to be the only reason these cops are sitting out here in the middle of the desert on a Wednesday evening. Yeah, that *has* to be the reason. Except the cops do not accelerate. They are hanging back from our pack of cars, about a quarter mile behind, as if waiting. Or observing. But what could they be waiting for? We begin to converse in our curiosity.

Immovable.

"I wonder if they are out here looking for alien Satanists who just escaped from Area 51," Randy says, in his quintessential childlike sarcasm.

"Hmmm. I'll bet they hang out here during the week nabbing illegals. I know if I had just crossed the border, I would head straight for the desert. It would be last place I would guess the cops would look," I answer.

"We should slow down and let them pass us, so we can follow them on their chase," Alex adds in typical, curiosity-killed-the-cat Alex fashion.

As the words are leaving his mouth, we spot a third and fourth 5-0 in the median just ahead. We pass them, and they just sit. They sit, that is, until the other two catch up to them, after which they fall in line behind them. The pack of four now cruise a quarter of a mile

behind us. Alex looks over at me with a conniving grin. He takes
his foot off the gas slowly, and the fuzz begin to gain on us. Only, in
our commitment to observe the flocking police activity behind us,
we have failed to notice that the other cars that were a part of our
convoy not sixty seconds earlier have now fallen back considerably
from us. We are alone. I look to the side view again and watch as the
cops overtake the vehicles who were with us, passing them without
seeming to pay them any notice. We are by ourselves, in the desert,
far from anyone and anything civilized, with four police vehicles
in pursuit. And they are gaining now. We are silent, not wanting
to acknowledge that they could possibly be coming for *us*. No way.
Impossible. This is our day. This is *my* day. Freedom. We are kings.
Immortal, invincible. Nothing would dare disturb our dream of
permanent tour. Yet, the unspoken thought is this: If none of us three
admit out loud that these cops are actually coming for *us*, then they
will just pass right by us and go about their business. Suddenly I wish
Alex hadn't taken his foot off the gas. They are now no more than a
hundred yards behind, and gaining fast.

"I think you should pull off the freeway right up here and let them
pass," I say. Immediately, as if they somehow heard me speak the
words, we are engulfed in a beam of blue and red.

Did I mention the fact that we are in the middle of nowhere? Did
you ever read that Steven King novel about the maniac cop in the
middle of the desert who pulls people over and then plants weed
on them just so he can have an excuse to drag them back to his jail
house, where he maims them methodically before finally murdering
them? Valid questions for my captivated audience at this point. Valid
because I am currently in that novel. Or at least I think I am. They
have their blinder beams on us as we pull of the highway at the next
exit. One 5-0, apparently the leader, is on his megaphone, talking to

us as we sit in our idling vehicle. He does not approach the van.

"Put both hands in the air outside the windows. Keep your hands where we can see them! ALL OF YOU DO IT NOW!" There is no soul in that voice. Only a mindless rendition of every authority figure that caught me trying to steal, trying to cheat, trying to lie as a seven year old. It is amazing how much our early memories come back in times like these, making us feel like children again. Alex and I exchange glances at this, eyes wide and glaring, mouths inadvertently hanging open as if gravity were pulling with a physical hand at our bottom lips. "Now SLOWLY turn the engine off and throw the keys to the middle of the road," the officer commands.

Invincible.

Immortal.

Freedom.

Now, it doesn't take an Andrew Schwab to realize we have just left the realm of normal protocol. I don't know about you, but most of my police encounters in the past did not begin like this. Bright lights and megaphones, maybe, but no tossing of keys and "hands where we can see them" talk. I suddenly understand how important my little freedoms are to me—the freedom to sleep in on a Saturday or the freedom to choose whether or not to vote. It is amazing how quickly our definitions (and priorities, for that matter) can change in a crisis. And, boy, are we in a crisis. Then suddenly, irrevocably, my dreams of being far from home seem like the most retarded things in the world. I would give anything, ANYTHING, to be back home where it is safe. ANYTHING to be near comforting, calming, mundane normalcy. Forget tour. I will work the 9 to 5 I have been running from, Lord. Just get me out of here alive. I will even stop making fun of my band members, I promise.

I wonder if these cops like men. I wonder if they have done this to their rape victims before. And from there, the path of my thoughts goes down an unimaginable spiral (at least up to this point in my illustrious twenty-two years of existence), conjuring up pictures of a brutal slaying in the desert with CUTCO blades and Craftsman drills. And the worst, most nightmarish part of it is that in the desert, no one can hear you scream. Yup, all else aside, we are at their mercy, and I pray to GOD Almighty in heaven that He has mercy on us at this moment. But, oh yes, kids, it only gets worse from here.

Alex now takes his right arm out of the summer air outside and brings it back into the vehicle to acquiesce to the officer's command—i.e. the killing of the engine and the tossing of the keys. As he brings his hand in, however, the cop blisters our ears with a brutal warning, which nearly causes me to lose my lunch and my last soft drink in one quick spurt:

"KEEP YOUR HANDS WHERE WE CAN SEE THEM! WEEE WIIILLL OOOPPEN FIIIIRRRE!!!" Alex is trembling, and I am too shocked for any emotional expression whatsoever. He thrusts his hand back out the window, flustered and quaking.

"How do you expect me to turn off the engine with both hands out of the window?!" He sounds like a child who has been told to stop crying, but who has been asked in the same breath if he would like something to REALLY cry about (this glaring contradiction in terms is something that has always perplexed me; it seems that parents and cops are somehow a part of the same authoritative hypocrisy).

What is Randy doing, you ask? Why, giggling in the back seat, of course. He seems to think this isn't real, that we won't soon have our heads blown off in a bloody massacre. I do not share his optimism at the moment, however. And it is about to get much more serious in the next few moments. The chief po-po then begins with his list of debilitating demands, now that our van keys have been tossed safely to the middle of the deserted road on which we are sitting.

"NOW. KEEPING YOUR HANDS IN THE AIR, WE WANT THE DRIVER TO EXIT THE VEHICLE." Alex complies shakily. I am watching him sidestep through the driver side window.

"NOW STAND WITH YOUR FEET SHOULDER DISTANCE APART, AND INTERLACE YOUR FINGERS ON TOP OF YOUR HEAD." Alex pauses and looks over at me before compliance, creating just enough of a space in time between command and obedience for the cop to become even more irate.

"DO IT NOW, SON!! DON'T MAKE US USE FORCE!!" Alex's eyes drift from mine as he does what he has been told.

"NOW, ONE LEG AT A TIME, GET DOWN ON YOUR KNEES ... SLOWLY." Now I can see where this is going. Oh no. Here it comes:

"I WANT YOU TO LIE FACE-DOWN ON THE STREET AND EXTEND YOUR ARMS STRAIGHT OUT TO YOUR SIDES, KEEPING YOUR FEET SHOULDER DISTANCE APART. THEN I WANT YOU TO TURN YOUR HEAD TO YOUR LEFT. THEN *DO NOT MOVE.*"

Over the course of the next five minutes, which seem more like five hundred, Randy and I go through the same terrifying process. Now my band is lying face down on a deserted road, in an ironic loss of freedom that is so completely fitting and humbling, considering my overwhelming desire for the liberty, which was to be this day. God moves in mysterious ways, you remind me. No joke.

Immovable.

Am I to learn one final lesson here, kissing the concrete, before I meet my Maker?

Most assuredly.

Was my heart in the wrong place today when we left?

Yup, no doubt there, my friend.

Is that why this is happening?

Right again. Hey, you are getting pretty good at this.

Are these cops divine messengers sent to claim my body as a lesson to a generation of purposeless dreamers, pursuing stardom to avoid having real jobs?

Good question, I'll get back to you one that one.

Am I being punished for being so impatient with the quirks of my other band members?

Oh yes, that's for sure.

It is amazing the questions *and* answers you can come up with when your rational mind goes bye-bye. My inner dialogue spins over and over again like a KROQ programming hour. Now I can hear a song by a band called Failure running through my head. It starts off with the words, "Say hello ... to the rug's topography. It holds quite a lot of interest with your face down on it." At this moment, I am anything but free. I am not my own. I belong to these fine members of the law enforcement community. Everything I have been given is a gift, to be cherished and appreciated, because I never know when it will all be taken away. I realize these things right here, right now. Why didn't I see this before? I am too shocked to cry, too mortified to speak, too humiliated to breathe. This is how it feels to be a Beta fish, corralled in a tiny bubble of glass for the world's amusement. I don't want to die. Forgive me, Lord. I was wrong to be such a freaking jerk today. I was wrong to be so selfish. I was wrong to desire this band as a means to my own human ends. Oh please don't let them be murderers or rapists or molesters or Eagles fans.

I hear footsteps coming my way from behind, and then a knee presses into my back with all the weight of the officer behind it. I hear a metallic *chick-chick* inches above my ears, which can only be the sound of one thing: a shotgun. Nice. Amazingly enough, I am no more frightened than I was before I heard it. I guess fear has limits, and in my case, I have pegged out in a completely numbed shock bordering on comatose. I am now handcuffed and being yanked (quite indignantly, I might add, to say the least) to my feet. His grip around my upper arm is staggering, as if I had any intention of even *thinking* of struggling in the first place. He pulls my wallet from my back pocket and begins to spin me around. Then, Alex opens his mouth as he is being cuffed.

"You know, if we could just talk about thi—"

"THERE WILL BE NO NEGOTIATION!" The chief answers. Invincible.

Alex does not make the mistake of opening his mouth a second time as we are led into the blinding white lights of what is, most assuredly, the end of our lives as we know them. One last time I begin to pray: Lord, I am sorry for all I have done wrong in this life, and more aptly, on this day. I promise if You get me out of this, I will NEVER, EVER be cranky again. And I will even offer to unload the band gear FOREVER if You get us out of this in one piece without a felony record.

Then, the cop begins reading us our Miranda rights. "You have the right to remain silent ..."

This is really happening. I am really here. I really am cuffed and sitting in the back of a squad car in the middle of the freaking desert. THEY ARE NOT KIDDING. I, Andrew Schwab, upstanding citizen, college graduate, adept public persona, and future leader of the free world, am now bound and locked in the back seat of a patrol car. I have never been handcuffed before, and there are a few things I would like to acknowledge to the world before my life ends in a few moments. I would like you to know something I have learned. Handcuffs *hurt*. They make certain these ten pound weights are as tight as possible on your wrists, so as to leave as deep of an impression as possible. And having your arms bound behind my body is probably the most humiliating thing that has ever happened to me. It is as if the long arm of the law does this to make it abundantly clear that you are completely and 100 percent at their mercy, and they can make you eat dog turds if they so desire to. Pleasant thought. I wonder if that will be the next step in the application of due process to we three prisoners. I wonder.

I watch as the cops deliberate, running our licenses and discussing possible torture options out the front of my squad car. They seem to be debating quite intensely with one another as to how to handle us. Maybe, just maybe, the locks on our doors are broken. Then maybe, just maybe, the desert shroud could hide us as we make our quiet getaway. I glance over to my right and see the door lock, then ask myself the obvious question: How would I pull up the lock—with my teeth? My head falls forward in dismay and complete defeat, once again reserving myself to the divine ordinance of the situation. God, I know You are there. When they kill us, let me go first, and don't let it hurt too badly. Have them put the gun barrel in my mouth instead of blowing my kneecaps off first. I know this sounds selfish, Lord, but cut me a break here. Just don't let it hurt. I know I have let You down miserably today in my attitude, and I deserve to die in a bloody heap of carcassrotflesh bludgeoned, abandoned, and unrecognizable even to my dear old mother. But please help us. And one more thing: If my mom does find out how we died, please don't let her find out that I missed my last scheduled visit to her house because I was watching basketball at home. Okay, Lord, I know You hear me. Amen.

It is at this point that I begin screaming the same four-letter word over and over again that my publisher won't let me print here.

I lift my head and look to the right. The next car over is home to our drummer, Mr. Alex Albert, who I have affectionately nicknamed "Plow" because he is our resident tough guy who functions as a wrecking ball in most situations, physically and emotionally. But right now, the look on his face is both pathetic and terrifying. I have never seen anything close to it on him. His mouth is half open, and his eyes are wide, his eyebrows peaking on his forehead. His jaw still hangs open, as he has apparently lost the wherewithal to contract the muscles that normally keep it shut. This in mind, I wonder what other muscles he has let go of in that squad car. Suddenly I am thankful that I am alone, and that each guy is separated in his own holding tank.

And then I notice something that will later be denied, and that very something is the irony of ironies, and will be the source of one of the greatest debates among the members of my band for years to come: I think I see wetness on the sides of his face. I squint my eyes and try to get a clearer picture of his face, which is almost impossible in this light. Yet, I would place a good wager on my first observation. This, from our fearless mercenary, our fullback, our devastating mass of two hundred thirty pounds-plus of drummer. It doesn't seem like something to laugh at right now. Nothing seems remotely comical at this moment. The apparent tears on Alex's face only make my heart pump in my chest with more urgency and utter panic. If Alex is this scared, how should I feel? What should I think? It is at this point that I look over at Randy, two cars away to my right.

Now, everyone has their own way of dealing with things. My way is to analyze every possible outcome of the situation so as to avoid any possible surprises, through the lens of conspiracy and panic. There is a fate worse than death. That fate is disappointment. If you can navigate the treacherous trail of life by avoiding disappointment, then gosh-golly-gee, you will be a happy man.

At this point, I am resigned to accept my death, so I can prepare myself for the pain of that bullet when it enters my skin. That way it won't catch me off guard, and thus, I can deal with overcoming my fear in the meantime. Oh, and did I mention I get a bit critical in the process as well? I tend to get a little negative when my life is being dangled before my eyes. Take away my free will, and bitter words spurt from my brain. The gift of gab is the gift that I have.

On the other hand, there is Alex's way. He is a weapon of mass destruction, a wrecking ball, an instrument of torture. He deals with life the way Godzilla deals with Bambi. I don't know how else to explain it. To him, life is series of events to be conquered and crushed. His way of fixing electronic devices, for example, is by hammering them into submission with his fist, and it usually works. But in this case he has been corralled, and frankly, I have never seen him in this vulnerable of a state. I have never seen any situation, event, or problem come into his destructive path that he wasn't capable of beating to a pulp both physically and metaphorically. Now he is a helpless baby rhino that has been cornered by the master hunter who is equipped with an elephant gun.

Then there is our old pal, Randy. Now, Randy is the laughter-is-the-best-medicine guy in the bunch. This makes for good times at wedding receptions and birthday parties, and ladies just loooooove his smile, which beams at all times. Randy is currently laughing at Alex and I, as our collective countenance has obviously spiraled beyond definition. Randy, on the other hand, giggles and smiles, acknowledging neither our pain nor his certain doom. Between you and I, I am most envious of his ability to dismiss even the most dire of situations as a joke. Somehow his wires have been crossed to the point of no return, and I can envision him someday being faced with an armed intruder in his home and responding by laughing so loud that it drives the intruder out of his mind. Then, the would-be assailant retreats, howling into the night. He is the guy that snickers his way through a painful ordeal and buries every last amount of true emotion deep in his interior. Think of that video for "Black Hole Sun" by Soundgarden, where everyone's faces are so happy it is SCARY. And he has a laugh so loud that it can keep you awake at night, even when it is four doors down the hall and you are trying so desperately to get your allotted eight hours of sleep. Currently, he is covering his mouth and bouncing up and down, no doubt struggling with all his limited might to contain the volume of his fit so the fuzz don't hear him. Oh, how his mother must have ripped her hair out while raising him.

Are we not an adorable bunch of would-be stars, basking in all the glory of tourdom?

Invincible. Immovable. Immortal. Freedom. All words I used to say. Now they are jokes that inmates will tell one another just before they catch me dropping the soap.

Now, for the moment of truth. The cops finish their meeting outside the cars and split up, approaching each of their respective units. They have not dropped their weapons. They are not smiling. They do not appear to be very happy to be "hanging out" with us out here in the wild, wild West. They do, however, seem to be coming to each of us for a reason. One of them comes to my door, opens it, reaches in, and reasserts his viselike grip on my upper arm. He then yanks me from the car in one fluid motion, as I stumble to maintain my balance in the process.

"Come out here, little man. It seems we need to have a word with you and your bandmates."

What is this? My desperate fear returns anew, announcing its presence by sending neural messages to the muscles in my throat and stomach. They both tighten simultaneously, and suddenly I feel a deep acidic sensation, like someone has just poured Liquid Plumber down my esophagus. Note: Acid Reflux Disease affects millions, and its primary trigger is stress. This fact is not apparent to me during our current cop episode, and I am now convinced that if the cops do not end my life, it will not matter, because the juices on my inside will burn a hole in my body regardless of how fast they pull the trigger. The cop drags my tense frame forward to the front of the car, where my band members are standing in a line. The other police officers have their side arms holstered but still unclipped, while my guy holds his in the hand that isn't grabbing me. He nudges me forward to stand in the line next to my boys. Apparently we get some last words before our assassination.

And we were going to be so great. We were going to do so many things. We were going to move mountains and change the face of music as we know it. But now, here, in the desert heat, we will crawl and meet our ends not with a whimper, not with a bang, but (Mr. T.S. Eliot, *eat your dead heart out*) with both a bang *and* a whimper (let it be known that I am not the one whimpering here ... that role belongs solely to our manly drummer. Okay, well, maybe he is not *whimpering* per se, but he is definitely even more scared than I am). Here we stand, cruel world, not going down in a blaze of glory, but handcuffed and helpless, one with an acidic, bitter frown, one with an "oh-face" of panicked neurosis, and one with a childish, mocking grin. Mom, I am sorry I wasn't an accountant. You warned me. I didn't listen.

"So, do you know why we pulled you over?" one officer asks.

"No, we don't," I say, looking down and away from their faces.

"You have no idea?" a second one asks.

"No, officer, we don't," Alex responds.

I am still clenched as tightly as a constricting python from head to toe, and I am refusing to believe that this experience will result in anything short of death. This is it. The payoff. The climax. This is the moment where the would-be heroes meet their bitter end, and the crowd sheds endless tears. This is the part where the audience is robbed of their happy ending, asking for their nine dollars back on the way out of the theater. Here we go. I am ready, Father. I grit my teeth and close my eyes, preparing for the absolute worst these guys have to offer. I clench even tighter, if that were possible, the very threads of my entire being quivering and ready to snap. Here comes the payoff …

Then, without warning, Randy inches forward in the line, turns his back to the officers, and drops his laser pointer to the ground at their feet. Do I have to remind you he is smiling while he does it? The cops explode in a fit of laughter that makes Randy's laughter seem like chuckles in comparison.

"Do you guys know that we got a call from a trucker saying we had a hostage situation in a large, maroon van?" one officer asks. "Apparently one of them thought the one in the back seat had a laser-scoped pistol and was holding the other two of you hostage. You can imagine what we thought we were going to be dealing with here. And one more thing, boys: It is a felony to point one of those things in someone's eyes when they are driving. Consider yourselves lucky to be free and free of charge."

The next thing I know, the handcuffs are being removed, and I am free again. I stand there, glaring at the cops for a brief moment while rubbing my wrists to try to regain circulation. I am still too worked up to do, well, anything rational. I blink my eyes. My stomach and throat are still clenched. I was ready for death, and now I am not dead. This will take a few moments of getting used to. Not dead. No buckshot in the brain. No felony record. No blindfold and last words. No machete massacre.

I have been given my life back. Okay, so I am willing to admit that possibly, maybe, just maybe, I overreacted a bit out of fear. Then again, me? Overreact? Noooooo. No way. Then, relief and thankfulness begin to set in, along with a slight twinge of embarrassment, which, when acknowledged, becomes painfully more than just slight.

We sprint to the van, our home, our sanctuary, free to leave. Somehow it does not feel quite like the safe haven I felt it was before this little incident. Somehow we will leave a part of ourselves here. We will leave a piece of the quiet naïveté that truly believed nothing could harm us out here, on the road. We leave a piece of our superhuman selves behind, as we learn for the first time as a band (and maybe as people) that we are not heroes destined for unlimited success and a life free of all accountability. We are, in fact, mortals who are in dire need of learning many a difficult lesson. We left our homes just hours earlier believing that this trip symbolized the end-all-be-all to human existence, and instead we were held at gunpoint with our very manhood (if nothing else) hanging in the balance.

As the fear and embarrassment subside, the excitement returns. But it is not the same. Sure, we have a couple weeks of shows, which will be amazing. And sure, we will create memories and perhaps a life for ourselves that no one around us believes is possible. But it is now less romantic. Somehow we all know it, though we may not admit it. This is not the end-all-be-all. This is a gift. Maybe I don't completely understand how it all works, but I know one thing: We are no safer from the cares of this world out here as we are at home.

And right as rain, not more than five minutes into our drive, the three of us begin (as men often do) to debate who was the most scared of the crew, as a sort of masculine ritual of domination. Honestly, if we were dogs, we would have been bouncing around the inside of the van at this point, pushing each other aside wildly to see who could urinate on the greatest amount of upholstery.

"Alex, I could have *sworn* I saw you crying in the back of that car," Randy begins with a snort.

"Yeah right, man! You WISH I was crying. Someone had to keep calm as they interrogated us. I was ready for anything. You guys were the ones panicking. I saw it in your faces," Alex responds in the quintessential defensiveness that is so Alex. He is truly offended at the thought that he, the man's man of all men's men, would *ever* shed a tear in fear. Randy and I exchange glances and roll our eyes.

"I don't know, Alex, it sure did *look* like you were crying," I add in a tone that is 150 percent juvenile in its sarcasm, as if I were really saying, "Somebody made a pee-pee in their pants."

"Whatever," the drummer states, trying to convince us and himself that he does not care what we think about the matter. In the end, we would have this debate at least 176 times over the next several years.

Our arguing ceases as quickly as it started, with the drummer shaking his head, and the pompous lead vocalist and his coyote-like sidekick retiring to the back. We lay side by side. I stare out the window at the heavens. They stare back. Somehow I know, once again, that what I consider to be ends in and of themselves are only means. So many of the things I turn into ends are just means. Means to a greater end. The greater end of me. Though the freedom I felt this morning is now tainted, I know that it is for good reason. Or at least I remind myself of this as I attempt to fight off the ripped-off feelings that crowd my insides. I want to be free. I want to write my own ticket. I don't want to play by anyone's rules but my own. But I know I can't. There is this voice haunting me, and it keeps repeating the same thing in my head, over and over again. I have no choice but to succumb to it.

There is no freedom in this world, this life, apart from Me. Think about this the next time you see one of those stupid laser pointers at a gas station.

CHAPTER 3
THE WORST DAY IN THE HISTORY OF PROJECT 86

CHAPTER 3
THE WORST DAY IN THE HISTORY OF PROJECT 86

AT THIS POINT, WE ARE GOING TO JUMP AHEAD IN OUR career, because I thought this next story would make a good chapter three, even though it takes place five years after the last chapter. To sum it up, in the five years between chapters two and three, nothing eventful happened. We just put out three records, sold more than two hundred and twenty thousand copies of them, and did seven national tours, opening for bands like P.O.D., Linkin Park, Taproot, Sevendust, Trust Company, and many more. After our first release, we signed to a major—Atlantic Records, who released our second and third records in conjunction with our independent label, Tooth & Nail. At the time of this chapter, however, we are labelless and looking for a new home, struggling to keep the band afloat after leaving Atlantic Records early in 2003.

Man, are we late. What a shock. We have to be in San Diego for sound check in fifteen minutes, but it is rush hour, and we are a minimum of two hours away here in Costa Mesa. Of course, Alex was tardy, and I could not reprimand him for it, because his excuse, at least in his own mind, was completely legit, as always: "Schwab, I don't want to hear it. Becca's sister's dog had a seizure today, and I had to drive it to the hospital. No one else could do it. It was a family emergency."

By this point in my career, I have developed a thicker skin, and instead of blowing my top every time Alex makes us late to a show, I just calmly and coolly punish him through passive-aggressive tactics. For example, when he falls asleep in the van an hour before we go onstage (which is his ritual), I wake him by banging his own snare drum next to his head. Yes, I know. I am so cruel.

So our van is basically destroyed by now. It has seen many battles and has fought valiantly, but it now has more than two hundred and seventy-five thousand miles on it. We haven't even driven it for the past three years, since we have been touring in buses. But now, after parting ways with our major label, Atlantic Records (and the tour support which came along with being signed to a major label, allowing us to afford to tour in a bus that cost seven hundred bucks a day to rent), we are back to touring in a van until we find a new label home. It is late 2003, in case I did not mention it. We are seasoned veterans. Yet, we haven't toured for the past six months because we fired our manager, and our current interim manager doesn't know his own head from a hole in the ground, to put it nicely. So I have basically been taking up the management reigns the past several months, setting up a few local shows to keep us busy. Which brings us to today. We are playing a show in San Diego to celebrate our own independent Internet only release, *Songs To Burn Your Bridges By*. I have gotten many a compliment on that title. I guess I am the master at turning whining and complaining into utter genius.

So, little do we know, as we pack the van at Alex's house in Costa Mesa, that once again, we are in for an adventure of biblical proportions.

Oh, joy.

The van won't start. Alex forgot to unhook the battery cable the last time we drove it, so I have to run to Pep Boys to buy a new battery. Swell. See, the maroon monster has a wiring problem that drains the battery, and it's not worth it to us to spend the money to fix it since it's on its last legs. Therefore, we usually unhook the battery when we are finished driving it. I use the term "we" very loosely here, because I am really only referring to one high-maintenance, unbelievably absent-minded member of my motley crew of musicians here. Just moments ago, myself, Randy, and Alex were inside the beast, ready to bolt, when we hear nothing but ... *click, click, click ...* as the key turns.

"We must have forgotten to unhook the battery cable when we drove it last," Alex says to me, knowing full well who drove it last.

See, here's the thing about Plow: Whenever I forget to do something or make a mistake or come unglued or threaten our A&R guy with intense bodily harm, the personal pronoun "you" is used by him in reference to Schwab's latest blunder. However, when Alex leaves his drumsticks at home on a fly date or somehow forgets to order T-shirts for a show or trips over his tom while unloading, cracking it and costing the band hundreds of dollars, the plural pronoun "we" is used in reference to the mishap. Let me give you a few more examples, just to make sure you get my drift:

Example #1:

Schwab: "Alex, where are the stickers I told you to order months ago?"

Alex: "Oh *we* must have forgotten to order those. I will get right on that next Monday."

Schwab: "I reminded you four times, and sent you two emails."

Alex: "Dude, I can't handle this right now. My sister's brother-in-law just came down with the measles, and Becca and I have been over there all day taking care of him. Just chill out, Schwab. It's no big deal."

Schwab: "But Alex, we need those stickers for tour. That's like one thousand dollars we are losing."

Alex: "Calm down, Schwab. It will be okay." (Schwab crosses arms and plots to depreciate the thousand dollars out of Alex's nice new pickup truck with a sledgehammer.)

Example #2:

Schwab: "Alex, did you remember to ask for those last two weekends of March off from work for those shows that were booked?"

Alex: "*We* can't ask for that many days off, Schwab. *We* need to make money to pay the bills."

Schwab: "Plow, you knew about these shows months ago. You will have to just work it out because the shows are already set."

Alex: "Any way *we* can reschedule them? I mean, I am just trying to make a living here."

Schwab: "NO WE CAN'T RESCHEDULE THEM. I REMINDED YOU ABOUT THOSE SHOWS A HALF A DOZEN TIMES!"

Alex: "Calm down, dude! *We* can call my boss right now and get it off! Geez!"

(Alex has forgotten to ask for the days off, and in his embarrassment is trying to cover his tracks rather than solve the problem. Meanwhile, Schwab rushes to the emergency room for treatment on his ulcer, which has gotten much worse in the last five minutes.)

Schwab returns with the battery on schedule, of course. We place the battery in the maroon monster. It is now 4:30 p.m. Our sound check was a half an hour ago, but no matter. We don't need a sound check, because we are Project 86. And despite our lack of focus off the stage, we tend to completely destroy things when we are on it. Now. We are set to meet our bass player, who has been off doing who-knows-what all day, about fifteen miles south on the freeway. So we leave, drive up Alex's street, and start heading south on the freeway. All is safe, calm, and bright, heading toward another show in our illustrious career.

At least it is calm and bright for all of five minutes …

The van begins to rattle violently, not five miles south of Alex's house in Costa Mesa. Who knows what this means, but I am optimistic about the fact that we will make it our eighty miles to the show. Oh yeah, why would anything go wrong?

"Guys, this doesn't sound good," Alex says in his typical paranoia.

"We'll make it. It's just an old van," I say.

"I don't know, dude. I think we should turn around and go back to my house. We can take my truck and Steve's to the show. I'll call him and tell him to drive north to meet us at my house." As much as I hate to admit it, Plow is almost never wrong about these types of things. I mean, I am as much of an auto mechanic as I am a construction worker. I don't even have calluses on my hands, believe it or not. In other words, I am not the expert here. Alex says we have a problem, so we have a problem. We head back to his house and wait for Steve. It is now 5 p.m. We are onstage at nine.

We are now just waiting for Steve. Beating rush hour is now completely out of the question, but no matter. We can still get out of here by 6:00 and make it to the club by 7:30, with plenty of time to chill before we play. I am not stressed. I am an a-okay. I am the pillars holding up the great coliseum back in the days of the Roman Empire. Alex, Randy, and I sit outside Alex's house throwing rocks at each others' faces while we wait for our elusive bass player. Then Alex's phone rings.

"Hello … what? What?! Are you SERIOUS?" Alex exclaims into his cell phone. Uh-oh, this doesn't sound good. Not good at all. "No way, dude. Are you okay? What are you gonna do? On no. Dude … Are you serious? Man … Okay. Call us back when he gets there." Randy and I are just standing there, staring at each other, knowing full well what we are about to be told as Alex hangs up his phone.

"Dude, Steve got into a really bad car accident. I guess some lady rear-ended him on the freeway, and he is waiting for the cops to come right now, a few exits south," Alex says.

"Is he okay?" I ask.

"He says when she hit him, she was going like forty, and he was at a dead standstill. I guess his neck and back are totally jacked, and she has no insurance."

"So now what?

"When the cops get there, he's going to call us back."

Steve has to be literally losing his mind. I mean freaking out. An upset to his comfort zone is akin to a death in the family. I'm not exaggerating when I say this. Steve is the most guarded person I have ever met. I mean, he's the type of guy who never gives you a hint about his personal life, never returns a phone call, never invites you over to his house, never even tells you his opinions on anything, unless it has to do with music. His family, his girlfriend, his thoughts, and his emotions are all basically one huge mystery that is painstakingly perpetuated by Steve himself. And this is all a very strategic and intricately designed plot by him to keep everyone out of his comfort zone, thus maintaining a safe distance between himself and any possible inconveniences. In his mind, ties to people in terms of intimacy equal threats. That's why he keeps everyone at bay, especially his band members, whom he is forced to be around. You can only imagine the type of threat we represent to him ... especially one abrasive, communicative, relational lead singer.

Now, many of Steve's acquaintances do not even know as much as I have written in these last few sentences about him. And I certainly wouldn't know this much if it had been up to Steve. But I, being the persistent, insightful, and analytical individual that I am, have concluded that Steve's strict and seemingly bizarre adherence to maintaining distance from everything and everyone is the perfect challenge for a little analysis game by yours truly. And this is a game I have been playing with Steve since the beginning: I push his comfort levels with everything from probing questions about his bathroom habits to little pokes in the side with my finger when he isn't paying attention. And not surprisingly, this makes me his secret nemesis, which is an attitude he shares very privately with my other two band members. Of course, I would never know any of this if I wasn't slightly skilled at reading between the lines. But, believe it or not, Steve's biggest Achilles' heel, however, is not his weird sense of privacy. It is his commitment to being the most well-liked guy in every single situation.

See, when you are committed to being the nice guy, you can never hurt the other person's feelings. You can never have outbursts. You can never really show any true emotion, either. You basically have to walk on eggshells all the time, so you don't offend anyone, ever. Your reputation as the nice guy can be sabotaged by one lapse in character. That's fine for him and all, and it really doesn't hurt anything until a real crisis comes up, and he has all this welled-up emotion from never really letting it out around his peers because he is so quiet and reserved all the time. He probably would not like me very much if he knew I knew all this, but I have this vague suspicion that no one in my band will ever read this book, so let's just keep these thoughts between you and I, okay? This brings us back to now. I feel bad for him right now, honestly I do. Steve is not a very flexible guy, and he does not deal well with any inconvenience. He is probably pounding his head on the concrete and ripping holes through his arms with his fingernails on the side of the 405 freeway. I just hope he is in one piece, emotionally as well as physically. And I really, really hope he can still play.

Now there's a little secret about the importance of the show tonight: If we don't get down there, sell some T-shirts, and collect our meager guarantee, I won't be able to pay my rent, which is due in three days. The band has been off the road for eight months, recording and looking for a new label home, and while we have been not playing shows, we have become increasingly starved. Last month I got a small royalty check, which saved me. And now it sounds like this month, the bow is finally going to break. Enter anxiety, tension, and panic into one high-strung lead singer. But how to you insist on making it to a show when your friend and band member was just massacred in a car accident? Just then, Alex's phone rings again.

"Hello? Yeah ... Are you serious? No way, dude ... Are you sure? Steve, c'mon, man you don't have to—Well, alright, if you say so. See you in a little. Later."

"So what's the deal?" I ask, completely hoping to heaven above that Steve is going to be a trooper and play the show.

"He says his truck is running okay. It's just dented in the back, but he doesn't think he should take it to San Diego. He thinks he can play the show, even though he is super jacked. I guess his whole right side is a little numb. So, what I say we do is figure out which tire on the van is acting up and change it. We don't really have a choice. The van has to get us there. We'll pick up Steve on the way. Come on—we don't have much time if we want to make the show at all."

YES. Despite the obvious stupidity of doing anything physical after a bad car accident, Steve is going to save my life tonight and do the show. I owe him one, for certain. Maybe I should delete those paragraphs I wrote a few minutes ago, you know, the ones that describe his personality quirks? Nah. It's easier to ask for forgiveness than permission, I always say. I'll tell you what, Steve, the next time I am tempted to follow you around a gas station parking lot spitting peanuts at you to harass you when you are on one of your many twelve-hour, mysterious phone calls, I will resist. You have a "Get Out of Jail Free" card.

The first thing we have to do is find a jack. It seems to me we used to have one in the back of the van, but when we check back there, it is nowhere to be found. So we grab the jack out of the back of Alex's pickup, and it looks like it couldn't even lift a Vespa off of its kickstand. But it's all we have, so Plow thrusts it under the maroon monster and begins cranking. After about four minutes straight of what seems like the most labored jack-cranking I have ever seen, the underside of the van hasn't even lifted an inch. So, Alex decides to force it, of course. There are so many reasons we call this man "Plow." Reason # 764 is that his solution to the dilemma of the square peg is to punch, smash, pound, and pummel until it fits into the round hole. The next thing I know, he is screaming at the jack and kicking the crank until it almost bends into a ninety-degree angle. Yet, somehow he gets the thing to work, and the wheel is just barely high enough off the ground for Randy and I to begin taking off the tire.

"Do it ... fast. I can't hold this very long!" he grunts, holding the jack so it doesn't slip. Randy and I are giggling and having fun at Plow's expense, which is our normal way of dealing with almost any awkward circumstance in the band. In fact, it is pretty much the time Randy and I get along the best; Randy and I are BFFs when we are having fun at someone else's expense. We are spinning the tire iron at light speed when ...

The jack slips.

Oh no.

And Alex's hand is under it.

Oh no.

And I see it all happen in super slo-mo high definition flatscreen reality. The rear axle groans in warning. Randy and I accelerate our crank pace. Alex's paranoia gives way to utter panic on his nervy face. He strains to hold the tiny hunk of metal in balance. The rear axle groans again, this time louder. Alex screams for us to hurry. Randy and I get defensive and scream back. Then, the heavens come crashing down all around us, focusing all their wrath on Alex's right hand, which is the only thing between two tons of weight, a tiny fulcrum, and the pavement. He shrieks in unison with the ripping crash of the maroon monster's return to planet earth.

"AAAAAAAAGH!"

And for a few maniacal moments, Mr. Alex Albert's hand appears to be trapped under two tons of steel.

Oh no.

I am frozen as he fights to free his captured digits. Randy and I yank the jack upward with super-human strength, praying that Alex's fingers don't stay lying on the blacktop when he pulls his body away.

And it doesn't move. And Alex is yelling in my ear to get him out. I can hear him yelling for his mom, his dad, his girlfriend, and even God for help. And the jack still doesn't move. And Randy and I are now heaving, threatening to rip our own arms out of our sockets in order save the hand of our poor drummer. It has now been one and a half seconds since the van fell, and I am seeing our whole band fall to pieces quite literally before my eyes in the form of severed fingers.

And Alex screams …

And Randy heaves …

And Schwab shrieks …

And Alex cries …

And Randy moans …

And Schwab, for a split second, reaches a point of clarity, a moment of fleeting inspiration in which, under the strain and duress and fear and flash of his entire existence, and the existence of his band, and all he is, and his very spirit and livelihood and manhood and soul condense and twist, his mind and aura leaving his body as he looks down on himself from a few stories above, floating like a phantom as the man he once knew is being stolen away by a freak accident which cost his drummer and friend the use of his right hand and the loss of four fingers, thus finishing this potentially world-changing band in one fell swoop …

And then the jack moves, and Alex is free …

And Schwab's spirit returns to his body as he sees that Alex's fingers are all there, still attached …

And Alex screams dirty words at the top of his lungs as he shakes his hand in the air, hoping that his fingers are still functional, hoping to inject some breath of life back into them with the motion …

And we all hold our breath collectively, not wanting to utter a single sound, not wanting to disturb the universe in these crucial seconds where our fates may be decided ...

... For how could we continue on with a crippled Plow?

We couldn't.

And he continues to pace and shake and curse and stare at the sky in writhing, inhuman agony.

And we wait, hoping his physical pain will abate.

Because if it doesn't, we all know there will be no show. No future. No anything.

And then I take the earth, the planets, the stars, and the fate of all humanity on my shoulders, into my own hands, as I break the silence and speak: "Alex, are you alright?"

He breathes through his nose, uttering a prolonged groan with his eyes and mouth closed. He says nothing to me besides this. Then, like no one else can, he answers me in his native Plow tongue.

He makes a fist with his right hand, winds up, and punches the side of his house harder than I have seen anyone punch anything, ever. Then he turns around, with blood dripping from his knuckles.

"I am fine. Let's get this stupid tire changed and get out of here."

And now we are driving again to meet Steve. We changed what we thought was the tire that was causing the vibration, and now all is fine, at least so far. The promoter called, and I explained to her what was happening. She was not happy, but what could she do? We managed to get a real jack from a neighbor, which made the change fast and easy. Alex has a huge bandage on his hand, but he is still driving (old habits die hard, don't they, Plow?). It is now 5:38 p.m. Steve is two exits south of where we are now, waiting as we approach minus vibration. Now all we need to do is grab him, and we are on our way. I am relieved as I sit and watch the buildings pass in the back of the van. Relieved? Yes. Yes, I am, because I know in my heart that we have gotten all of our drama out of the way for today. Relieved like you are after that first good puke in the twenty-four-hour flu, when you think you just ate something bad, and you don't really know that you are going to be dry heaving for the next twelve hours.

When we see Steve, he is obviously shaken. He sort of rolls out of his truck, unable to move his head or neck, and when he stands outside the vehicle and tries to walk, his back is so warped that his one shoulder is about six inches higher than the other. He limps toward the van, looking like the poster boy for Scoliosis awareness. His steps are slow and telegraphed, as if he is testing each inch of concrete below his feet for mines. This is not good. He opens the van door and tries to step in, but nearly loses his balance because he can't swing his foot high enough to step inside. I catch him before he falls and carefully drag him inside.

"Whoa, Steve. You are pretty jacked. What's the deal?" I say.

"I can barely move my neck or my legs. The stupid lady that hit me was literally going forty and didn't even slow down. I was stopped on the freeway. Her car is totaled. I am going to the hospital tomorrow."

"Are you sure you don't want us to take you to the emergency room right now? We didn't realize you were in such bad shape."

"No. I want to play the show," he says.

Done. We are going to San Diego. Gimped, crushed, and bloody, we are going to play our show. It is now 5:52 p.m.

Four more miles down the five freeway, in Mission Viejo, the van begins to violently shake again. We are silent, not even acknowledging that anything is awry. I, for one, don't care how much the freaking thing shakes as long as we get there. But it is getting worse by the second, and I am currently watching the entire world through a shaky, blurry lens. I look to my right and see trees passing in a fuzzy haze. My ears tickle like I am holding a vibrating pager to them. Then all of a sudden …

POP!

There goes the tire. It flaps lazily against the undercarriage as Alex fights to get across four lanes of rush hour traffic. I moan audibly, wondering what sins I committed today to deserve all this. All I really want to do is just pay my rent. Is that so wrong? We pull off to the exit, hoping there is a tire place nearby that will offer its services at this hour of the evening. Luckily, we are in an area that has several options. So, we steer into the nearest tire and lube facility, and I exit the van. I run into the office and begin to accost the gentleman behind the counter.

"Can you help us? We are a band on our way to a show in San Diego, and we have to get there FAST! We need a tire—we just got a flat," I say.

"Let me take a look at it and see if we have the right size. You guys are lucky. We are closing in five minutes," the dude says to me.

He makes his way out and checks the tire, then runs back into his garage and disappears. I look around, and every single member has disappeared down the street, no doubt calling all of their girlfriends. This is the standard in a crisis. Everyone scatters and calls their girlfriends. Because my girlfriend is this stupid band, I have no one to call. So I sit on the curb with my head in my hands, waiting for the mechanic to come back.

Seven minutes pass. Still no guy. Still no sign of my band, either. I wait, alone. Alone.

Finally, the man comes back and shares the news.

"Sorry, friend. We have nothing in that size. Nothing at all."

"So is there anywhere else that might have a tire right now?" I ask.

"I don't think so. We are open the latest of anyone around here."

"Thanks for nothing," I say, bitterly.

"No problem," he responds, apparently not schooled in the art of listening, wit, or sarcasm.

Now what? It is about ten minutes after six, and we are soooo screwed. And of course, I can't find my band. I run out to the street in the hopes of catching some glimpse of them. Way off in the distance I see Steve walking further and further away from me. As for Alex and Randy, I have no idea. I return to my place on the curb and place my head in my hands once again. Remember when I said that we had gotten all of this out of our system only an hour earlier? I stand corrected.

Finally, the boys return some ten minutes later, expecting the tire to be replaced. I inform them that we had no such luck and that we had better think of something else, and fast. So, we get back in and start the engine, then proceed to hobble back the way we came on three good wheels. We haven't a prayer in the world. We are dead.

As I wallow in self-pity, we continue to drive around the city of Mission Viejo on three good tires, looking for some glimmer of hope in the form of a twenty-four-hour tire place. We pass three or four places that are closed, and with each successive "closed" sign we pass, my heart sinks a little lower. Oh, Mom, you were right all along. I should have been an accountant. Or maybe even a lifeguard. I am going to be on the streets begging for rent money tomorrow. Maybe I can sell some autographed pictures of myself on eBay. I am sure if I sell a couple hundred of them, I can pay for half a month's rent.

Then, at the bottom, in the pit of mire and filth, like a beautiful stream flowing in the middle of the Mojave desert, I see it. Is it a mirage? Apparently not. There is a tire place right up the street in front of us, with a sign gleaming the magic word. No, it's even better than a magic word. It's a heavenly word. It says, "Open." It is now

6:57 p.m. Don't forget, we go on at 9 o'clock sharp, and we still have an hour and fifteen minutes of driving ahead of us. Well, what do you know. According to my math, which is usually flawless, we have almost a half hour to get the tire changed. Perfect. God in heaven is real. Anyone who tells you otherwise is sorely mistaken.

As it turns out, after talking to the guy at the tire place, they have one set of the size tire we need, and all it will take is sixty minutes to put the thing on. At this information, I stand in the corner of the service office pounding my head against the wall like Benjamin in *The Graduate*. I have coined that move and made it my own now. Several families with small children are watching me in awe and horror as I do this.

"Mommy, why is that man hurting himself like that?" one kid asks.

"Son, you shouldn't look at that man. He is very scary, and this is a great lesson in why you should not talk to strangers. There are a lot of crazy people in the world, and they will hurt you if you even make eye contact with them," the mom responds.

I am proud, as always. My spectacle of grief is a powerful teaching tool, even when I am not onstage. I continue to pound my head in the corner for the duration of the next hour, until our van is finally ready to go again. Where did I go wrong? What happened? How did we get here? I remember having such high hopes, but here we are. All of these sinking feelings have built up in me over the past few months. I have watched our bank account drain as our band has become increasingly inactive after parting ways with Atlantic Records after our third record, *Truthless Heroes*, was abandoned by them. I have sat at home making phone calls day after day for the past month in the hopes of replacing our manager and business manager, whom we fired recently just after we parted ways with our label. No luck. Few promising leads. With no one to spearhead our operation, we have played few shows. And I know that even though no one will admit it out loud, every member of the band is contemplating calling it quits. Everyone except me. But I feel powerless to keep the ship from sinking. This is all so hard. Alex is getting married in less than a year, so he went out and got a full-time job, which conflicts heavily with playing music full-time, of course. Steve has a girlfriend in Amsterdam, which consumes his every thought, pulling and distracting him from his musical commitments as well. He spends weeks on end over there, away from rehearsals, songwriting, and shows. And Randy, oh Randy, bless his heart. He works as well, even though his heart is in the band. But he is so easily distracted that he has been putting his time into his side band because there has been nothing going on with Project 86. I can feel it coming apart right now, here, before my eyes. Maybe it is just time to end all of this.

I had hoped that tonight, our first show in weeks, would be a rekindling of the love.

Nope. It is 7:52 when we get our van back.

At this point, I feel that our day would not be complete without a huge argument with Alex. So, I decide to take all of this out on him.

"Plow, if you had taken care of maintaining the van instead of procrastinating, none of this would have happened," I say. Silence for a few moments. He is just shaking his head while he drives. This is not the response I am looking for, so I continue. "I mean, I know you are busy and all with your new career, but some of us still care about this band." There. That should do it.

"Are you kidding me, Schwab? Tell me you are joking right now, because if you aren't, then I am going to pull over so I can SOCK YOU IN THE FACE!"

"Oh, I am serious. It just seems like your mind is on everything else but this band. Why don't you just say that you don't want to play with us anymore? It is so freaking obvious by your actions that you don't care." Oooh. This is going to be the granddaddy of all Schwab/Plow bouts. Randy and Steve are silent, of course, both lacking the courage to interject anything in the middle of the two warring superpowers of planet Project 86.

"Schwab, you have got to be the most insensitive, selfish person I have ever met. I DON'T CARE ABOUT THIS BAND?!?! HOW COULD YOU EVEN SAY THAT?! ARE YOU A COMPLETE MORON?! YOU HAD BETTER JUST SHUT YOUR MOUTH RIGHT NOW!!!"

This is our little dance we do, Alex and I. He tortures me with lateness, forgetfulness, and overall neurotic behavior. So, I torture him back by pushing his buttons. He drives me nuts because he *is* nuts, and I, in turn, try to make him more nuts. We have been doing this for years, and nothing much changes. This time, though, it is serious. I feel like I have a valid point, and I might as well make it known now to make sure we hit rock bottom at this very moment. Alex has recently given his schedule over to a full-time job, mostly because he is getting married in a year. This is valid and all, but it still doesn't change the fact that we are still a band, and we have to be available to do things like record and tour. But he can't do any of that at this point in his life because he can't get the time off work. He has officially taken himself out of the game at this point, and I am ticked off about it. I haven't told him how ticked off I am up until this point, so now is as good a time as any. It's almost like I really want to test *everyone* right now by provoking them. You know, to see how badly they really want to stick with this whole thing. There is no better time to take the temperature than when the heat has been turned up. And right now, the whole building is on fire, and we are contemplating jumping from a ten-story window to escape the flames.

"Alex, I will not shut my mouth. I know you are getting married next year and all, but that still doesn't change the fact that all of us are in this together. We never discussed getting full time jobs or waning in our commitment to the band. We are just in a dry season, but it's going to pick up again. I guarantee you, we will get into a new label situation and be able to make more money doing this than we ever have in the next year. BUT YOU JUST GAVE UP AND GOT A JOB THAT YOU CAN'T GET OUT OF!!! YOU EFFECTIVELY SCREWED US ALL WITHOUT EVEN TELLING US!!!" I am really mad. Can you tell?

"SCHWAB, I AM GOING TO KNOCK YOU OUT RIGHT NOW. I CAN'T FREAKING BELIE—"

"BELIEVE IT. We all feel like you are bailing on us, yet you are so wishy-washy about ever giving us a straight answer about your situation. You say you are still doing the band, but your actions say something else. I can't even get you to commit to anything more than weekend shows. WE CAN'T EXIST AS A BAND ONLY PLAYING ON THE WEEKENDS!! We need an answer from you. Are you in or ARE YOU OUT?!!"

Alex is silent, no doubt so angry that words can't form on his lips. I know I am being a jerk, but I can't help it right now. I either need to start collecting alternate career options, or I need to get a commitment from my drummer. There is no other way. If we were a different outfit, getting a new drummer would be an option, but our band just doesn't function that way. No Plow, no band, in essence because we are a team, and no one in this band would move forward with this thing without the other three. That's why this current scenario is so freaking horrible. I mean, I know for a fact that Alex can't help his situation and he is not to blame. I know this thoroughly. But I need some one to scream at here, and Alex is my chosen victim, as usual. I just never expected this day to go like this. I never meant to take these things out on my drummer, and I may have just murdered my band. If you are reading this, sorry, Steve. Sorry, Alex. Sorry, Randy. I only want this whole thing to work, and if we all would just be men and buck-up, we could avoid a lot of this silliness. In the meantime, back to Alex …

We pull off the freeway in silence, and I have never felt more like our band is finished than at this second, right now. Alex exits the van and punches it (really, really hard—honestly, I would never want to fight him, because it would hurt, and BAD), leaving a huge dent in the driver's door. Then he starts kicking the radiator, denting it as well. Steve is moaning, and Randy, for the first time in his life, is not laughing. I am just staring off into space with a stupid look on my face, not knowing whether or not I just killed our baby.

I am an idiot.

It is 8:20. We are on in forty minutes, and we still have an hour or so left until we get to the club. I call the promoter, this nice girl who works for House of Blues, and who also just so happens to be a big fan. I assure her we will be there soon, get her up to speed on all the mishaps of the last few hours, and she says it's not a problem. She says she will just make the opening bands play a little longer. Of course, though I tell her these things, I am convinced we will not be playing at all again, ever. We are through. Alex is pacing outside on his cell phone, and now Steve has joined him. Randy and I just sit there, not knowing what to do or say. This is the end, for sure. Over, out.

Ten minutes pass. It seems more like ten hours, mostly because I have been watching Steve and Alex pacing on their cell phones the whole time. It is frightening to witness all of this, frankly. It is even more frightening to think about what is to become of my world after the events of this day. This band is pretty much all I know, and the thought of moving forward without it terrifies me to no end. It's like the thought of splitting with your mate. Though they are the thorn in your side and drive you absolutely out of your mind, the void that would exist in their absence is unfathomable. These are the thoughts that rush through the mind of someone who has spent their whole life holding onto things they are afraid to lose. The irony in thinking this way is that when you actually do lose those things (which always happens, inevitably), they are torn away from you, because your grip is so tight. The end result is far worse, because the ripping process takes a part of you with it. Welcome to Schwab's world of destructive thinking. I am glad I am not the one who is ultimately in control here.

And with that last thought dangling in my cranium, the miraculous happens: Steve and Alex reenter the vehicle, silent but calm. Alex starts the engine, and for a brief second, I fear he is going to take the north onramp and head home to call it a day. He drives toward the freeway, the south ramp on his right, the north ramp a little further up on his left. The fate of the known world is now out of my hands, and the whole thing hangs in the balance of one simple decision. Do we go north or south? I am praying, and praying hard with my eyes shut. Oh please, don't let it end today. Not this way. Give me another chance to make it right. I will even apologize to Alex for my earlier statements. Just one more chance to make it right. I open my eyes.

We are headed south, in absolute silence. A sober smile creeps over my face.

We do not speak the rest of the way down there. I am still left wondering what is going to happen when we play, if we play, if we *can* play. We arrive and are greeted by three hundred kids and a packed house, which is a great Band-Aid for the sores. People still care about our band. We load in, working together as a team to get the gear onstage so we can hurry up and play. I watch as Steve tries to lift his bass gear, and it drops from his grasp time and time again like Jesus stumbling on His way to Golgotha. This is going to be very interesting. Maybe we will all collapse, here, tonight, on this very stage and throw in the towel. I help Alex with his drums, but we still don't speak. I am still really upset, part anger, part sadness, part sinking feeling like something inside me died on this day that I will never be able to regain. I stand backstage as my band line checks, waiting for Randy's opening guitar line, during which I make my entrance onto the stage. I am doubtful; I am weary. Do I really want to spend any more of my life pursuing this?

Then, Randy's guitar starts playing, and I walk onstage, head down. Chills run up my spine as the cheers are deafening. I almost forgot—I don't have a choice. I have to be here. I have to perform. It is written in my D.N.A. This stage is my home. Oh please, let the dream continue for just one more night. Tonight. I look at Alex as we start, making our first eye contact since the great battle of 2003 … He hits the open high hat harder than I have ever seen and winks at me. I scream longer and louder than I ever have in return.

If I have said it once, I will say it a thousand times. You could have a stomach virus, the mumps, a dying grandmother, and hemorrhoids all at once, and there is one thing that is guaranteed to make it all disappear. You could have just been attacked by a rabid dog and be gushing blood from multiple flesh wounds, and there is something that will put the pain in its place. You could even have the worst day in the history of your band, and there is one thing that will cure it all.

What is that one thing?

Playing a show.

Now, don't get me wrong here. Steve can barely move, Alex is still bleeding out his knuckles, and our relationships with one another are on the brink of divorce, but it is all put in its place on this fine evening at Soma, in San Diego, California. There's something about drama that conjures up the dredge in each of us so we can spew it out on that stage. And when it comes out, it comes with force, blasting the audience with our problems, fears, insecurities, pet peeves, and anger. And when you are finished, you feel holy and right.

I look to my left during the first song, and I see Steve rocking harder than I have seen him in ages. At another point, I make eye contact with Alex, and we smile at each other, knowing that we are each apologizing to one another in the best way we know how: during a song that we are performing, communicating to one another telepathically. If I didn't know better, I would say that our connection tonight to one another and the music is exceptional. And I am sure no one in the audience has one inkling of a cue what has happened to us today, besides the fact that we were thirty minutes late getting onstage. I can't help but feel that everything is going to be okay. My rent will be paid, as usual. There will be no homeless begging in the street, no applications for new employment. I am proud to say we will live and make it through one more day, one more show, and probably beyond. One more season. I know this because, well, I just feel it.

I can't stand these guys most of the time, and I am sure they can't stand me, but we will push on from here. These are my friends no matter what happens, no matter how much we battle. We will make a new record. We will talk about our problems. We will find a new label situation, a new management situation, a fresh start. We will live again.

Mark my words.

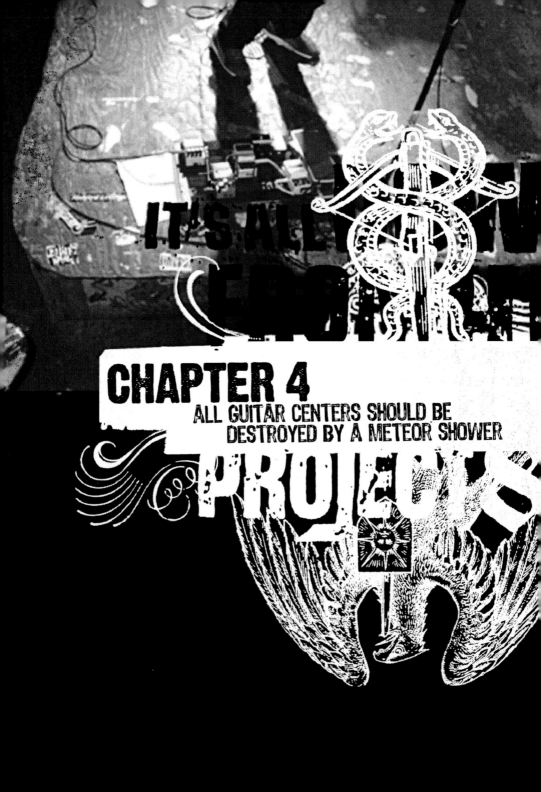

CHAPTER 4

ALL GUITAR CENTERS SHOULD BE DESTROYED BY A METEOR SHOWER

CHAPTER 4
ALL GUITAR CENTERS SHOULD BE DESTROYED BY A METEOR SHOWER

IF I EVER MEET THE GUY THAT INVENTED THIS CHAIN OF stores we are going to sit down and have a little talk. I think the idea of having a huge nationwide chain of music stores is great, in theory, because in any given town when we are short on strings, sticks, or drum heads, we know we can go there and find what we need. I think that's cool, and I am all for it, obviously.

But somehow all Guitar Centers are structured—from the bottom employee to upper management—to waste as much of your day as possible, while subjecting you to inhuman musical torture. On top of this, every time I have ever been to one, I have noticed that although there are at least 7,523 employees at each location who seem to be doing nothing more than jamming on the latest Trace Elliot amp or Pearl drum kit, they can't ever seem to find the time to offer any service whatsoever to their customers. And every customer service guy, when you actually do drag him kicking and screaming away from his vintage, used Stratocaster, with which he was so accurately covering "Desperado," he always fits the same mold—a loud-mouthed, opinionated, failed musician who is in seven cover bands, but can't seem to locate the one piece of gear you came to buy. And when he does locate those strap locks your guitarist needs so desperately, they always seem to be in the back warehouse, at least twenty minutes from reach. Never mind the fact that we are in a hurry. Never mind the fact that there is a kid in the drum section who hasn't quite learned to play a 4-4 beat, but man, is he sure hitting those things hard and loud, and I think I may snap at any moment if that guy doesn't get back with those strap locks.

Now, some of you may enjoy the cacophony of seventeen different out-of-tune guitars hammering and soloing along with four different drum kits and twelve different basses all at full volume, while waiting for two hours for what should take no more than four minutes to buy. I, for one, do not. Therefore, I have come up with the following list of suggestions for the executives at Guitar Center:

1. Place volume limiters on equipment. This will cut down on the number of violent crimes that take place in the neighborhoods surrounding your stores, committed by patrons who are at the end of their ropes to begin with.

2. Place time limits on equipment that is being used. I suggest three minutes, which is the longest solo that Eddie Van Halen ever played in a song. And when explaining this limit to customers, remind them that Eddie Van Halen only needs three minutes to decide whether or not he likes the sound of a particular guitar.

3. Only hire employees who have decent taste in clothing, music, and art. I know this will require a massive layoff of staff, but in return, you will be equipped with a workforce who will discourage

silly customers from flooding our world with more noise and eye pollution. Consider it Guitar Center's contribution to the environment, specifically the cultural and mental environment. This means you can't hire anyone who owns an Eagles record. This means you can't hire anyone who worships Rush. This means you can't hire anyone who remotely resembles Sammy Hagar. Or anyone who appreciates the work of The Allan Parsons Project or Jimmy Buffet. On the other hand, if they can appreciate The Clash in all their splendor and glory, then they may be worth hiring.

4. Make a very strict policy that employees may not, UNDER ANY CIRCUMSTANCES, play with the merchandise. Tell them the reason for this is because they want customers to have a pleasant day. If they break the rule, do to them what they did back in the old days: Cut off their hands as a warning that they will be fired if they do not comply with employee guidelines.

5. Soundproof a room, and place a TV in said room with a decent selection of Playstation 2 games, assorted magazines (none having to do with guitars, basses, drums, or Sammy Hagar), and have a few beverages ready. This room will be for lead vocalists like yours truly who absolutely lose their minds when in the store. This place will be called "The Soothing Room" for obvious reasons.

All this having been said, I feel that it is only fair to mention the fact that Guitar Center has taken care of us very well over the years, particularly our friend Jason Vanderpool, who has worked there since the very beginnings of the band. I mean in no way for this commentary to seem like indulgent complaining from the prima donna lead singer that I am. In fact, I also would like to point out

that this little session of suggestion has little to do with the fact
that I am slightly defensive about the fact that I do not play an
actual instrument, even though every time I go to Guitar Center, I
wish that I did. No. This has nothing to do with these things. I am
merely pointing out, as a consumer, that there are some very urgent
dilemmas facing the Guitar Center franchise, which I know can be
easily remedied. Thank you for your time and consideration.

CHAPTER 5
HALITOSIS

CHAPTER 5
HALITOSIS

HAVE YOU EVER NOTICED THAT PEOPLE WITH BAD BREATH stand too close to you? If you play music for a living, you will learn this cold, harsh reality. See, usually kids can get very excited to meet the people in the bands they admire. This in and of itself is not a bad thing. I thoroughly enjoy talking to everyone who comes to our shows, fielding questions, and developing deeper relationships with everyone who is inspired by the music. But for some reason, the normal, sweaty youngster (the one *without* the dog breath) has a healthy respect for the proper distance between two human beings in a conversation. On the other hand, the kid with the really, really bad poo breath has absolutely no comprehension of what is the proper distance between two bodies when they are speaking, like I said.

I guess the principle is obvious: If you have the common sense to take care of your breath, you will naturally have the common sense to stand far enough away from someone so that when you talk, they don't get a glorious whiff of your esophagus. And don't bother trying to step away from someone who has the death stench. These types must be heard at full volume (at least in their own minds), and they will gladly take one step toward you for every one you take away. And of course, you can't devastate them by letting them know about their smell. That would obliterate them and probably cause tragic emotional trauma that would be traced back to you for all eternity. So, when faced with a stinky dilemma such as the aforementioned, I usually just grin and bear it. I don't hold it against fans when they have the feces aroma when they approach after a show. It's almost expected by now.

But what if the roles were reversed? What if you met someone you admired, or who was famous, and *they* had horrible dog breath? It would shatter every pedestal you ever had them on …

So I get this call from our manager. It is sometime in the spring of 2000. We have been waiting for an offer to go on the road to support our second album, which will be released on Atlantic Records, *Drawing Black Lines.* And we are restless and tired of staying at home, so we have instructed our agent, as well as our manager, to put us out there with anyone, as long as it gets us on the road again (we had been at home for five months prior). It seems we have gotten a tour offer, and I am extremely excited.

"So who is the tour with?" I ask.

"Uh … you won't believe it," our manager says.

"Tell me!" I exclaim.

"Uh … are you sure you want to hear this?"

"YES! You know how bad we want to be on the road. It can't be that bad!"

"Well … you guys are going on tour with Queensryche."

Silence from my end at this. No freaking way. Oh man. That's almost so bad that it is great. In fact, I know it is.

"Wow. How did *that* happen?" I ask. "Does anyone even come to their shows anymore?"

"Believe it or not, they still sell out fifteen hundred-seat rooms every single night. They have a huge following of forty-plus hair metal chicks who haven't quite let go of the glory days."

"Count us in," I say.

The string of dates ends up being just that—a string. We are playing a handful of shows on the West Coast only in key markets like San Francisco and Las Vegas, mostly House of Blues in these cities (which rules because there is nothing like HOB catering), and a few theaters. We have an opening slot, like forty-five minutes or something, which should be cake. This is amazing. I remember hearing that song "Silent Lucidity" in like eighth grade or something, and making fun of it. But they were freaking huge back in the day. Huge. I remember seeing the singer, Geoff Tate's face plastered on the cover of every single music magazine. This is so wacky and random, yet kind of nostalgic. I wonder if these guys will even talk to us. I wonder if their wives are like twenty (no doubt, the band members traded in their antiques for newer, sleeker models). Then again, those dudes have to be at least fifty-five. I wonder if they all have arthritis and play to backing tapes. This is going to be amazing. This is going to be surreal. I hope I get to meet Geoff Tate, just for the story it will make. Oh, and what a story it would be.

So we show up at the first show in San Francisco (at the Warfield Theater) for our sound check and load-in. The Queensryche road crew is setting up their stage props behind us as we check our instruments. The crew seems pretty nice. Most road crews can be pretty hard on the opening bands, but these guys go out of their way to shake our hands and let us know they can get us anything we need. Wow. Classy. I look behind us during our check, and I notice all the props are advertising their new record, *Q2K*. Ooooh. No good. This is all going to be very, very interesting.

As we finish our check and leave the stage, I notice a guy in a weird top hat and tight-fitting, tapered black jeans. Oh wow. That has to be one of the band members. It turns out to be none other than the lead guitarist. He is standing with what appears to be his wife, a woman who was undoubtedly gorgeous fifteen years ago, with the pinwheel hairdo she is currently sporting. But now, ouch. Rough. You remember the pinwheel, right? When all the girls made their hair in the front look like the Whos of Whoville? It was like this huge competition in the '80s for who could make it the poofiest, the peacockiest. I feel as if I am going to be seeing many individuals in the next week who can't quite bear to part ways with their heyday.

Oh please, you who read these words, I give you a very important command: If I ever, ever, EVER become "that guy"—you know, the one who just can't seem to let go even though his pouch belly is protruding profusely through his faded Smashing Pumpkins T-shirt, and whose hairline has become increasingly frightened of his eyebrows, whose tattoos have all blended into a wonderful blue shade, and who must dominate every single conversation with stories from his heyday in rock music—if I ever become him, you MUST smack me as hard as you can in the face and scream in my ear for me to wake up from my pathetic, ridiculous dream. Everyone knows someone who is "that guy." He's the one who never got over his brief and futile taste of the limelight and whose every waking word has something to do with some story about when his band opened for blahblahblah. He's the one who plays in cover bands at age sixty-two. Smack me. Hard. Please.

I have now just realized that we will be playing for fifteen hundred of "those guys" who have come to sing along to a band made up of "those guys."

WOW.

The guitarist approaches me. He means to make contact. I extend my hand.

"Project 86, right? Man, you guys rock. We heard your disk and just had to have you guys come out on the road with us. We have never heard anything like you guys! How did you come up with your sound?"

I stand there, silently, long enough to make the pause in the conversation awkward, but there is just way too much to digest in what he just said to me. First of all, the guitarist from Queensryche loves my band. Second, he said that they have never heard anything like us. That's right, in the age of Korn, Deftones, Rage Against the Machine, and ten thousand other heavy bands flooding the market, they have never heard anything like us. Where do they live? In igloos? Third, he is asking me for musical advice on how to create a unique sound. I decide to roll with it because it is just too great.

"Thanks so much, man! I guess we just try to make music that fits how we feel. I really appreciate the compliment, and we are really excited to play with you guys."

"Yeah, man, we are so glad to have you. Please come join us down in catering after we sound check. I gotta run, but it was great meeting you."

We get to eat with them and share their catering food. I want to be on tour with Queensryche for the rest of my life. The band is all onstage now, and I am bouncing in my shoes, ready to explode because I am so excited about watching them sound check. Of course, the band resembles the mental picture I developed in my brain the second we were asked to tour with them, right down to the bass player's headset microphone and falsetto, pitch-perfect voice. The entire band is onstage now, all except for the lead singer, Geoff Tate. They run through a few "jams" from their new record, as I stand out front, listening to a completely perfect mix. I sure can give them this: All those years of practice have sure paid off. The mix is so dialed in, so crisp, so crystal and pristine that I can only sit there and be a little jealous that my band doesn't sound anywhere near this good. Of course, we are a much different outfit than them, and when you move as much as we do onstage, it's hard to sound as tight as you would if everyone stood still.

Then, out of the backstage darkness appears a dark figure dressed in black leather and black sunglasses. His presence commands the stage, even when it's just a pre-show sound check. He approaches the lead vocal mic, just as the band is breaking into "Jet City Woman," their mega-hit from the mid-'80s. Then, from his mouth comes that sound. That sound I remember hearing in the background as MTV blared every single day after school while I did my junior high homework. The voice careens off the walls of The Warfield in reverbial magic. He. Is. Geoff . Tate. His voice hasn't waned with age at all. He sounds exactly the same. Exactly.

Now, don't get me wrong here. I was never actually a Queensryche *fan*, per se. But how could you exist back in the day and not know who they were? Had to clear that up. I was into heavier bands like Slayer, S.O.D., and, of course, Metallica. Okay. Back to the point.

Fast-forward to the show, after a wonderful meal of filet mignon, which we ate with the "Q" road crew, another assortment of "those guys" who treated us to endless stories. We take the stage to a half-packed room, and I can feel immediately—within like three seconds at the most (I have incredible intuition for when a show is going to suck)—that we are doomed to a miserable and torturous fate here. Maybe it's the fact that not one single person, besides the seven kids in the back row wearing Project 86 shirts, make any noise whatsoever. Oh yes, I do not exaggerate. It is cricket, cricket.

I am standing with my back to the crowd, feeling the awkwardness that our music is going to create with a forty-plus audience. At that moment, I know it is going to be long forty-five minutes. We had never played in front of a crowd that just stared at us and kept silent up to this point in our career.

I spin to face the crowd as the first song begins, and I realize that it is much worse than I originally forecasted. Maybe "worse" is not the best word to describe it, because performing for these people, who probably will be completely annoyed—if not utterly wanting to murder us—by the end of our set, brings me a deep, sick pleasure. There is something about being onstage, forcing people to hear your voice because *you* are the one with the microphone. And when they don't want to hear it, there is something that drives me to get right up in their faces, nose to nose, and let them know that they are not getting rid of us.

I look to my left, and there is a girl wearing a bandana on her forehead, flipping me off from the moment we start playing. There is another guy sporting the coolest mullet I have ever seen in my life, doing the same. The three girls directly beneath me in the center of the stage are mocking me by giving me the thumbs down. I am loving it. I quickly skip to the side of the stage with the bandana girl, and she extends her finger right into my face as I lean down toward her. I am kissing her hand in between lyrics, during the song, as she tries to put her finger in my eye (it would turn out that she keeps her finger extended toward me for the entire show. Now THAT is commitment). After exchanging pleasantries with her, I make my way over to the thumb girls in mid-song. They are frowning at me. So, during the bridge of the song, I wave at them with a smile. I don't think I have ever had this much fun in my whole life. Then, I glance to stage right and give a friendly wave to the mullet guy, just as he hucks an empty Bud Light can at my head. I duck, and it flies by me. Then I blow him a kiss. YES, I LOVE THIS TOUR.

All in all, the show is a success. None of us get hit with any projectiles, and I manage to make what I hope is a memorable impression on all the middle-agers in the audience. We are the only opening act, so Queensryche will be up in like thirty minutes. You can feel the electricity in the air. Yes, that's correct. I said "electricity." It is the appropriate word, believe me. I am standing backstage at the moment, toweling off, and hoping to catch a glimpse of the "Ryche" before they take the stage in a little bit. I never thought, as a child growing up in Western Pennsylvania, that at age twenty-five, I would be doing this. And if you would have told me, I would have told you to … well, you know. The hilarity and irony and ridiculousness of all of this are massive.

But oh, you won't believe what happens next.

I am standing outside in the hallway by the Queensryche dressing room, trying not to look obvious, trying not to look anxious, when their door opens. Oh man, this is it. I see them each, in turn, trickle out into the hallway, talking to who appear to be friends and family. They are not walking toward the stage yet. They are just hanging out all around me. All I am thinking about is how I can't wait to tell this story someday. Then, I see Geoff Tate exit the room and come into the hallway with his wife. They exchange a few words, then Jeff glances my way, then does a *double take*. He is looking at me. At me? At *me*. He gives me the "what's up" nod and then begins coming my way. Oh, this is too good to be true. I feel my stomach tighten and a flash of cold dart down my frame for just a second, then I regain my composure. An ugly, yet unavoidable thought crosses my mind: I could sing "Silent Lucidity" as he approaches, pretending to be "that guy." I don't have the courage to do it, but it would have made for another great story.

And here he comes to talk to me.

"Hey, man, I caught your show. You guys have great energy and presence. I really enjoyed it. Come here, I want to show you something," He says, and turns around, meaning for me to follow. And I do.

It all happened so fast ... but something crossed my nostrils for a microsecond ... wait ... no way ... not him ...

No way. Not him.

I dismiss the thought from my mind as I follow, excited and curious. He leads me through the crowd of people backstage, past their dressing room, and around to the back corner of the stage. I follow at a distance, slightly timid. In front of me I see only darkness and shadow. He seems to be leading me down some kind of secret corridor. Maybe he means to show me perverse rock star things of which only the inner circle know. Visions of strippers, porn stars, heroin, coke, and strobe lights pass through my head. Is that what these guys do, even at age fifty? I think I am about to find out. The build-up is killing me. He continues to weave his way through black curtains behind the stage, and I fight to keep up. Then he disappears in front me. I panic for second, having no clue where I am or how to get back to where I was. Finally, I push my way through a final curtain and almost trip into a small, red-lit room.

What is this place? What in the world is he doing? The room is no more than a booth. I look around me, and there are a few shelves and mirrors. On the shelves are ridiculous amounts of personal grooming effects. There are blow dryers, hairsprays, mousses, gels, combs, scissors, colognes, and much, much more. I am staring. I can see him turning toward me to speak, but as he does, an earth-shattering, dream-crushing thing happens ...

No ...

No way ...

UGH!

As the breeze of his turning slips by my face, I am transported to another planet, one of trash heaps, outhouses, and people who don't shower. It is black in this place, like charcoal. I feel the frightening reality closing in on me here, and there is no escape. Only dark, warm, dank air and that ...

SMELL.

"This is my vocal booth. I wanted to give this to you. It's a vocal spray that helps lubricate your throat so you don't lose your voice as easily. Here."

I can barely make out his words, because I am too distracted. No. Nooo. NOOOOOO! He is standing too close to me. Way closer than necessary. I refuse to believe this, but ...

GEOFF TATE HAS HALITOSIS.

GEOFF TATE IS ONE OF THOSE PEOPLE WHO STANDS TOO CLOSE TO YOU WHEN TALKS.

GEOFF TATE HAS CHRONIC BAD BREATH.

I can barely speak, barely move. Famous people don't have bad breath. Just like really pretty girls don't go to the bathroom. Somehow, though, I am able to respond to his gesture of kindness.

"Thanks so much, man. And thank you for bringing us out on the road with you. We know it's going to be amazing. Well, I won't keep you long. I know you have to get onstage," I say.

"It's no problem at all. Anything you guys need, let us know."

Then he turns back to the curtain, and I think there is a green, iridescent cloud swirling around his head, trailing from his mouth, threatening to infect all in its path. The cloud bends and spreads as I follow, wrapping its evil tendrils around my face, forcing its way into my insides. I think I may puke. Geoff Tate, the lead singer of Queensryche, hero to millions, has chronic bad breath.

In the end, we had our fun annoying their fans, eating their food, and enjoying their shows. I knew it would make a good story. But, sometimes I have bad dreams. And in these dreams, I am at a rock show, backstage, while some shadowy figure is leading me through dark tunnels filled with the charred remains of aftershave and blow dryers. I follow the figure ahead of me, knowing he is leading me to unspeakable horrors that lurk just ahead of me. The tunnel curves just ahead, and around the curve, I can see a faint, green cloud, stagnant and macabre. I know I should turn back, but I can't. The monster or creature or beast or boogeyman or whatever it is that is leading me down the cave has some hold on me that I can't get away from. And as I round the curve, the creature turns on me. It has the face of an ashtray filled with skunk remains. And it sprays and sprays, attacking me with vapors of death. I shriek, but of course, no one hears me.

I awake in a pool of my own perspiration, realizing another ugly truth about our world: Even famous people have bad breath.

CHAPTER 6
BAND CREW GONE BAD, PART I

CHAPTER 6
BAND CREW GONE BAD, PART I

TIME: SPRING 2003. PLACE: A TRUCK STOP SOMEWHERE in Nebraska. We are on our way to a run of shows with Sevendust. We are in an RV instead of a bus or a van this tour. It's one of those mid-sized deals that seems like a cool idea until you get halfway across the country, and all the accessories that made you think it was a cool idea to rent the stupid thing in the first place are broken. Example? The TV went out like two days into our trip, and we have all these DVDs and a Playstation 2 to occupy us on long drives that we can't even use. We are very restless. There are six of us total on this tour. It is the four of us, our merch guy, and our tour manager/ sound guy. Needless to say, the six of have been jonesin' to get our hands on a new TV. It's all we have talked about today. And we intend to have one before the day is over. But as it turns out, there is a gap in understanding between the members of our band and our merchandise guy as to what is an acceptable means to obtain said TV. I have no idea what awaits me at this truck stop ... and what kind of trouble our merch guy is about to unleash.

Can I indulge you for a few moments in my thoughts about road crews? I will put the whole thing in perspective using a very cheesy naval analogy, so you can easily understand. Here we go: Your road crew is the group of guys that, for all practical intents and purposes, run the whole show on tour. They are, in theory, the ones who have the band's back in every aspect of operation. Think of them as the crew of a nuclear submarine, each commissioned with very specific duties to ensure the safe transport and maneuvering of a vessel with very important cargo. If you are out to sea in battle and someone blows his role, then your ship can very easily become one big BOMB.

First, you have your road manager. He is like the captain of the ship, handling everything from the overseeing of scheduling interviews, to maintaining financial reports, to informing the band on when and where they need to be, to threatening promoters with pain of execution if they do not pay the band what they are contracted to pay them. The road manager also oversees the entire crew and takes care of every last detail of your tour. Now, a good road manager makes you feel secure on the road. He is a leader, a charismatic figure, an amazing organizer, and a shark in making sure your band is taken care of in every little way, from backstage food to cash to hotel rooms. It is so vital to the sanity of your band that this guy is well-trained and trustworthy. Believe me—a bad road manager will stuff all your cash under his mattress and forget where your guitars were stashed after the last show. Then he'll pick fights with your bus driver and crew, resulting in paid help leaving the tour unannounced, leaving you high and dry. A bad tour manager will make your whole setup look pathetically unprofessional and leave out such details as, say, leaving lead singers behind in restaurant bathrooms, resulting in being embarrassingly late to important shows because the bus had to turn around an hour after leaving said lead vocalist behind. I guess I could write a whole other book on bad tour manager stories with Project 86. You get it. I will leave it at that.

Then, you have your stage manager. This is the second guy in the chain of command, like the XO, usually overseeing everything that happens on the stage, from setting up and tearing down to set lengths. We have never had one of these officially on the payroll because, well, we are not that huge as to be able to afford a stage manager. We have been on tours with stage managers, and they are very valuable in making sure everything from sound check to teardown runs exactly as planned. But these guys are usually the most annoying to deal with if you are in the opening band because they are schedule freaks. They will make you cut your set short if you are running even one minute over. Frankly, stage managers are usually insecure guys with power trips who have been placed on earth to make life difficult for every band except the headliner.

Next, you have your sound guy (FOH). Though he holds no official officer power in terms of running the show, he, as you can guess by his title, can has been charged with the duty of making you sound really good. Having a paid sound guy on staff, instead of a house sound guy, can make all the difference in the world. Ever been to a show where the band sounds like trashcans banging? It has as much to do with your sound guy than it does with the band. There are many who say in the sound arena that "you can't polish a turd." I disagree. The right sound guy can make a turd shimmer if he is so inclined. He is like the sonar technician on the boat; if he falls asleep in the game, the enemy may spot your naked ship and sink it.

And on and on down the line. Guitar techs. Drum techs. Lighting guys (LDs). The point I am trying to make abundantly clear is that your road crew is your livelihood on the road. They make or break you and your band. And they usually get paid well for it, an average of twice as much as band members. You wanna make money in music? Become a guitar tech. Become a road manager. I am not kidding. You see, the thing is, a good road crew is very rare and a very hot commodity. It is such a niche form of work, and there are very few of these guys to go around. This is probably because most crew guys want to actually be in the band, so they get sick of just teching. What can I say? It's not the road crew that the girls like. But the thing is, and I can't really figure this one out, the most fringe elements of society are somehow attracted to these jobs. And these fringe elements usually start out as merchandise people for bands, working their way up to tech and then later to road managing if they stick with it. But merch guys are typically the biggest characters, or in our case, the most dedicated troublemakers. And this brings us to our guy on the current tour, who is named Logan Shaw.

Now, Logan is a childhood pal of Alex. Alex has an entire entourage of childhood friends who are thugs, criminals, and all-around crazy dudes. I don't know the appeal, but this element has always lurked around Alex, despite the fact that Alex himself has never been that way, at least since I have known him. It should be known that though Logan is now and always has been a well-loved guy by all of us, including myself, when the idea of him coming out on the road was presented to me by Alex, I thought he was nuts. Note: my initial reaction was based partly upon another of Alex's cohorts who handled some crew duties a few years prior and who ended up stealing a few hundred dollars from the band. No way, Alex. Uh-uh. Nope. No chance. Logan is a great guy, and I love him to death, but I can just imagine the crazy things that will happen. I mean, I have heard the stories about him. Fights. Jail. Drugs. I tell Alex that there is no way over my dead body we are bringing him out. Yet, somehow Alex convinces me that Logan is over all his antics, that he loves the band and really just wants to do a great job for us selling our shirts. And the fact of the matter is that we have no merch guy for the tour. So, despite Schwab's concerns, Logan gets the job selling our merch simply because we have no one else. And he *does* do a great job … for the first few weeks of tour. We love having him out there, and he is about the most fun guy around, always making us laugh, always breaking the tension. Absolutely no bumps in the road until …

We all pile out of the RV and separate in classic fashion, our posse dispersing to various locations throughout the truck stop, where we hope to find a new TV. I walk with Randy as Logan trails not far behind. Everyone else enters in front of us and disappears into the restroom to deflate. As we walk through the front door, my eyes scan the room, looking for the first trivial thing that will absorb my attention. There is the usual Trucker Speed display (Ephedra is bad for your heart, but good for your creativity), the audio tapes rack, the hand radio aisle. My personal favorite staple of the American truck stop is the T-shirt rack. Every now and then, you can find a really cheesy "I brake for trucker chicks" shirt, or the ever popular "no lot lizards" (which refers to this legend of prostitutes who populate rest areas on the highway, going from truck to truck soliciting "jobs." I personally don't believe lot lizards exist because I have never seen one. But then again, I have never seen a Russian mail-order bride either, and I am pretty sure they exist), which is most definitely worth depleting your per diems.

I continue forward through the convenience store with Randy, and we both spot a big display of exactly what we came for: a cheap, fourteen-inch color TV. Yes. No more sitting in silence and boredom. We will be basking in the glory of *Grand Theft Auto* and *Halo* in no time. We will begin building our brand new Project 86 DVD collection, 2003 version, ASAP. I think our first purchase should be that movie called *Office Space*, a brilliant piece of work and a must-have for all those who despise the nine to five corporate office career rut that we are so desperately trying to avoid. Or maybe even *The Big Lebowski* or *The Royal Tenenbaums*. Any film will suffice actually, so long as we can all quote the words to each to each other as we watch, thus making the whole experience so much more of a collective. Randy and I look at each other and smile, then we look back at Logan and smile again.

"Should we get it?" I ask.

"For sure," Randy agrees, and we both smile at Logan.

"Logan, can you grab one of these for us while I go find Alex?" I say.

I am so excited. Alex has the band credit card, so we have to find him. Randy and I turn and walk away from the TV display to get him. These are the simple moments, though they would seem so far beyond trivial to outsiders, that make the road so worth it, so memorable. Sure, you wouldn't even remember the day your bought your last TV, and truthfully neither would I. Except everything seems to mean so much more when you are packed into a little cardboard box with wheels, traveling the countryside for endless hours, weeks, months. Experience is heightened. Everything means so much more. And though it is so much harder than your ordinary life at home, it is so much more crucial. So much more …

I glance over my shoulder, back at Logan, to see if he is behind us. What I see when I turn back around shocks me so badly I can't even move. Are you ready for this? Logan is running for the door with a TV on his shoulder, in plain sight of the checkout lady! He is stealing it, and she sees him doing it! Randy I are both so utterly baffled and terrified that we just stand there staring at each other with eyes the size of Disney characters.' What in the world are we going to do? We are going to jail FOR SURE this time. No time to yell at Logan. He is already gone out the door. The checkout lady eyes him as he passes, her gum dropping out of her mouth. She is probably thinking to herself that it isn't possible for someone to be that, well, retarded. Meet Mr. Logan Shaw. He is currently working on his doctoral thesis in petty larceny. He obtained his master's degree in criminal studies, and is currently in the editing phase of his first book titled *Warrants and Writs: A Classic Case Study in Legal Dilemma*. Oh, he's a genius. No, really, I am serious.

"Randy! Quick!" I yell. "You run and get the other guys as fast as you can and get them to the RV. We have to get out of here, NOW!! I will go get Logan and tell him to put that TV back! Oh, we are so DEAD!"

I sprint to the front door in an all-out battle to somehow find Logan. He had to have gone to the RV with it. Great. I can't even imagine how I will manage to keep from causing him serious agony if we get out of this. Oh, he is paying for all of our bail out of his pay and then some if we get caught. No, wait. If the cops come, we will just explain that he is a homeless guy we picked up along the way. Or maybe we can just leave him for dead. Yeah, right. There is no way we can just leave him here, no matter how much we have nothing to do with his craziness. I have to get to him and get us out of here. I reach the front, and the checkout lady is no longer behind the counter. Maybe she chased him out the front. I rush through the front door and back out to the parking lot, and almost annihilate the checkout lady, who is standing there gazing at our RV. I barely avoid the fatal collision as she is turning to re-enter the store.

"Tell your friend to return the TV right now," she says in a quiet tone that suggests we may already be done for. Did she already call the cops? I am praying. Praying again. How do we always seem to find ourselves in these dilemmas? No time to figure it out now. I just have to find Logan. I give the lady a dumb look as if to say, "I have nothing to do with this," but I don't think she buys it. I am standing on the concrete in front of the store, scanning the parking lot for him. I look over to the lady again, who has now made her way back to behind the counter inside. She is picking up the phone and looking out at me. And now she is dialing. Her eyes move from me to the RV again, as she is no doubt looking for our license plate number. There is no doubt in my mind that if we don't get out of here fast, we will be in jail tonight and for a very long time. I look back to my left, over to the RV, and see a sight that in retrospect is one of the most hilarious things I think I have ever seen. Of course, at this moment, nothing could make me laugh. What I see just makes me more furious and panicked.

From my vantage point, I can see a profile shot of the RV. I look to the rear of the vehicle, and underneath the back end just behind the rear tires, I see a pair of Nike Cortez running shoes. Logan's Nike Cortez running shoes. On the ground, just next to him, I can see the TV box in all its splendor and glory. Now, what makes this whole scene so amazingly ridiculous is the fact that anyone looking at the RV from the parking lot would see his feet and the box, plain as day, even though I am almost positive that he thinks he is completely hidden. He walked right in front of the checkout lady in an attempt to steal a TV, then found the most obvious hiding place in the whole world! I resume my sprint to the RV and round the side of it to find Logan standing there with an excited look on his face. I truly believe he thinks he has done the ultimate act of courtesy to our band, thus fulfilling to himself his divine call and mission as our merch guy.

"Dude, what are you DOING?" I scream.

"I thought you guys said you wanted a TV?" he says, obviously surprised at my lack of enthusiasm about what he clearly thinks was a genius move.

"Logan, you have to take that back inside NOW! The girl behind the counter is calling the cops! And why are you standing out here?! You can see your feet and the TV all the way across the parking lot!"

"I couldn't get back into the RV. It's locked."

"Go! Make sure you tell the lady that we had nothing to do with it!" I yell.

He picks up the box and waddles awkwardly, pants sagging, in an honest attempt to get the TV back inside the truck stop. Now it is a race against time. All I know is that we have to bail. My entire being is set on one purpose. Where is everyone else? Did Randy even find them yet? Each second, those sirens draw closer. Soon I will hear them. Each moment that passes is one moment less separating myself and my friends from a prison record. Oh, and these Midwest cops aren't as friendly as their Orange County associates. They don't like people who look like us. Tattoos, piercings, and black hair equal guilty as charged in these parts. No, they don't take kindly to outsiders here in the sticks.

I hide behind the RV (behind the tire, where no one can see, unlike my genius counterpart) and wait. Alex has the key, the *only* key. And they are nowhere to be found. Suddenly I am back in the desert again, lying face down on the concrete with a shotgun aimed at my skull. Suddenly I am in seventh grade getting caught for shoplifting a pair of sunglasses, my parents waiting outside the store for my interrogation to finish so they can ground me for months on end. That familiar feeling invades every inch of my skin, crawling, scraping, biting ... I am going to be in the back of a cop car on my way to a Nebraska jail cell, where I spend the rest of my would-be tour listening to stories from my new roommate named Sully, who is getting five-to-ten for crop smuggling and participating in the black market John Deere trade. Yup. This is it.

Just then, Logan comes barreling around the corner of the RV again—by himself.

"Where is everyone?!" I scream at him.

"I dunno. I went inside and put the TV back and then took off to come back out. I am sooo sorry, Schwab. That was stupid."

"Never mind that—we need to find them and get out of this state. I am going back in to find them. You wait here and stay out of sight."

I take off running (again) to try to find my bandmates. But just as I get out into the parking lot again, I see them come bursting out the front door like some cartoon version of themselves, falling over one another, arms flailing desperately. It looks like they are actually having fun with this. Well, that makes one of us. I spin around and get back to the RV door, ready to never come within five hundred miles of Nebraska ever again. When I return to the side of the RV, Logan grabs me.

"That was so stupid, man. What was I thinking? I am so sorry, Schwab, I will never do this again." Evidently he is afraid that I am going to send him home. I haven't even thought about it, if you want the truth. I just want to avoid going to jail. I just want to exit the Cornhusker state. And yeah, I do kind of want to choke Logan with a guitar string.

"We'll talk about it when we get out of here," I say with a flat tone. It's hard being a babysitter. It's even harder being a parent.

Alex, Randy, and Paul (our tour manager) round the corner of the RV. But there is no Steve. No Steve. No Steve. And you would think that I wouldn't be surprised. I am expecting to hear sirens in the distance any second.

"Where is Steve?" I ask, not concerned about the level of paranoia in my tone.

"He is a little tied up in the bathroom, he ate chili for lunch earlier," Randy responds. He adds a little chuckle for good measure, just to make sure that I am as ridiculously disturbed at this moment as possible. Yeah, now I am back at Tomfest in my nightmare, only there is no ketchup, and Steve is the one disappearing. Alex unlocks the RV door, and we all pile in like that human domino beer commercial. The engine is started, and I take my place on the back bunk, ready to man the rear lookout, but there is still no Steve.

Where is Steve? That is the eternal question as we await our demise. I can't tell you how many times that question has been asked in the history of this thing, and we now have a running pot for when, if you ask that question, you have to put in a dollar. It is currently at $7,643.00

The seconds pass, and we are running laps around the inside of the RV, panicked and looking out every window for the first glimpse of our bass player, who is MIA. Steve is always the guy who disappears. We actually have a rule that no one is allowed to utter the words "where's Steve?" We would go in and get him, but all of us are too afraid. We continue to bounce around the inside of the vehicle like Mexican jumping beans. This is ridiculous. How long does it take to handle your business?

Waiting ... Waiting ... Waiting for Steve in agony.

"How far is it to the next state?!!" I yell up to the front.

"We have eighty miles to go!!" our driving drummer responds. It has now been over five minutes since Logan originally bounced out of the front door of the store with the goods in hand. That is enough time for the cops to be on their way. Our one saving grace is that this little stop is the only remnant of civilized culture for miles.

I am praying, praying, praying. Oh, please, God, no jail, no cops.
Have mercy on us. Logan knows not what he does. Ever. I am just
wondering when all this good "karma" is going to run out on us. We
have been running up said karmic debt for over six years now. Not
that I believe in karma. Not that I believe in karmic debt either. Then,
we see Steve walking mildly out the door toward the RV, unaware of
the immediate danger we are in. We all scream out the window at
him in unison:

"STEVE!!! HURRYYY!!!"

"Alex, GO, GO, GO!" I belt in a more genuine *Another Boredom
Movement* performance than any I have ever offered from the stage.
The RV swings wildly left, throwing every piece of loose luggage,
not to mention every loose body to the right side of the vehicle.
Paul throws the door open, and Steve dives into the moving box-
on-wheels. His feet hang out of the swinging door as Alex continues
to swing left, heading for the onramp to Highway 40. Only three
hundred yards to the onramp to go. I see a row of tractor/trailers in
front of us, blocking our current heading.

"Alex, watch out for those trucks!"

"I see them, Schwab, just hold on, this is going to get crazy!" He
immediately jerks the wheel the opposite direction as my head slams
into the window above the back bed.

"AAAAH!" I scream in pain. The entire left side of the RV and
the trailer lift off the ground in the mayhem, and for a split second
the thought crosses my mind that I will be greeting the friendly
neighborhood Nebraskan fuzz from underneath a compacted
Winnebago. But the tires grip the asphalt, and the airborne side of
the P86 machine comes crashing back down to earth, sending Steve
tumbling out of the top bunk, four feet down to the floor. He screams
in pain, cursing Alex's driving.

And suddenly, unexplainably, I realize something: *We are having the time of our lives.* I start laughing from the pit of my stomach uncontrollably, looking at the scene of wildly piled bodies, trash, and luggage on the floor of the RV. I am the only one who is still sitting upright. I laugh and laugh and laugh. Logan's legs are in the air as he lies on his back on the floor with Steve and Randy piled on top of him. They are all screaming and wailing in pain, adrenaline, and joy. Just then the bathroom door swings open, and Paul plunges out, reaching for the door with his pants unbuttoned. That's when we all really start to lose it.

"Look at Paul! What are you doing, man?!" Logan screams from his bottom bread position in the current human sandwich scenario, pointing his finger toward the bathroom and almost to the point of tears. We all join in and point at Paul, as he fights with all his effort to regain his balance, hold his pants up, and shut the door all in one motion. In the process, he drops his pee bottle to the floor, and it splashes and bounces, barely missing the boys on the ground by inches. The spray flies just over Randy's head, splattering on the wall just past them instead. I feel tears streaming down my face as I can't even bear to look at this surreal scene. I put my head down and scream into the pillow that is next to me in complete comic agony. I think my stomach is going to burst. We may be going up the river, but we will go with side-splitting laughter if we do. The next thing I know, we have steadied and are rolling down the freeway again.

"Alex, what is the fastest this piece can do?" I shout to the front.

"I got it up to seventy-five yesterday."

"Well, get it up to ninety. We have a long way to go, boys. Keep praying. I am going to keep watch out the back for any 5-0."

Now that things have calmed down and we are back on our way, I realize: I think we are going to be safe. Call me optimistic (for once?), but I just feel like our laughter was an omen. I don't even think any of the other guys are that mad at Logan, though he obviously needs a bit of correction. In their eyes, especially Alex's, it is no harm, no foul, when dealing with a guy like Logan. I am still beyond perplexed as to what was going through his thick skull when he did it, so I want to talk to him. Should I let it go? Should I send him home? Should I dock his pay? Or should I take this as an opportunity to painfully apply the concept of forgiveness? Yet, forgiveness is perhaps the most difficult concept to obey, especially when someone has put so many things in jeopardy. My career, my livelihood, my sanity, was dangled above an active volcano just moments ago. Yet somehow, my anger has already subsided. I am watching the dotted lines on Highway 40 stretch out behind our trailer and dissipate into the Midwest oblivion behind us. No bright blue and red lights behind us this time. No lights at all. I can see a few miles back, and we are alone on the road.

"Logan, come back here," I call out. He bounces next to me, holding his head in his hands and moaning.

"I am so sorry, Schwab. I have no idea what was going through my head. I thought you guys wanted me to steal it. I really did. I know how stupid this was. I will never do it again. You have my word. I promise I will never do it again."

"Do you realize how much you put us in danger, man? You are our crew, our livelihood out here. You can't sabotage us. You just can't."

"I know. I am sorry. I really am. You have my word."

"If anything like this happens again, you will have to be the one who takes responsibility for it, you know? We have to keep this whole thing on course."

"I know. I would have never allowed you guys to get in trouble for this. I would have taken the blame, of course."

"Cool, we forgive you. Just please think about all of us before you act."

You may think I am crazy. But what is the right thing to do? I can only forgive him and hope he moves forward and doesn't hurt us. Somehow, I feel like this won't be the last time he lets us down like this, but I don't think he will ever try to steal anything again. It's strange, though. I feel like there is a reason he is out here with us, like we are all being protected from above, and he is to somehow see that. I don't think he will hurt us, though I think our patience will be stretched. Sometimes people are placed in your path to teach you these things, though it may not make much sense at the time. If you would have asked me what I would do if one of our crew members had put us into a situation like this one, I certainly wouldn't predict I would have reacted like this. I don't know. I just think that if we don't give this guy some grace, no matter how difficult it is, we are in the wrong. Besides, do you know how hard it is to find a new merch guy halfway through a tour?

MY FAVORITE QUESTIONS

Now, I am sure none of you really are aware of this, so I am going to take a page or so out of your time to save you (and myself) the awkwardness that would result if you did not read this next little section. I have titled this page appropriately. These are my favorite questions. In fact, I like these questions so much because they are so amazingly original and so utterly memorable that I felt I needed to share them with you so that every single one of you would know not to repeat them to me, and thus diminish their greatness and uniqueness. Now, you wouldn't want to devalue these questions, would you? Of course not. So, being the nice guy that I am, I am even going to provide you with the ANSWERS to these uncharacteristically genius and well-thought-out questions.

QUESTION #1- "What happened to your afro, Andrew?"

ANSWER- Well, hmm … let's see. First, I cut the wretched thing five years ago, just after we released our second record. So, you are a little late on that one because I am at least a half a dozen different styles past it. I grew it out in the first place because I had just lost my mind after barely enduring a very trying time in my life. So, I decided to stop cutting my hair. I got the bright idea to 'fro it out for a show, and hence the nightmare began. Honestly, I hated being a public spectacle everywhere I went because a huge round shrub was on my head. My band hated it, as well as my family. I hated it the most because it was impssible to maintain and it was very much not getting chicks. You obviously have not bought any of our records since *Drawing Black Lines*, our second release, because I had my hair like that when we recorded it in 1999.

QUESTION #2- "What does the dragon mean in your logo?"

ANSWER- Well, hmm … let's see. Our drummer chose the dragon because he thought it looked cool. We all went along with it because we thought it looked cool, too. We had no intention of any inherent meaning because we just thought it looked cool. The irony is that he never has to answer this question because he is a drummer and no one wants to talk to drummers. It was actually a well sculpted and intricate plan on his part to make me lose my mind.

QUESTION #3- "What does Project 86 mean and how did you come up with the name?"

ANSWER- Well, hmm ... let's see. We used to call our band "The Project." but then we thought we would come up with something a little bit more sophisticated, so we decided to put a number after it. We chose "86" because of the reference to isolation, rejection, and removal. It used to mean that identity is found in isolation, like the isolation that comes from standing up for something that isn't popular, thus causing rejection. Let it be noted that we thought the idea of a band name that consisted of a word and a number was revolutionary back in 1996. Now I would say the idea has been slightly diluted, if not completely corroded. Oh, and by the way—it has nothing to with the last time the Bears won the Superbowl.

QUESTION #4- "Don't you have another guitarist? Where is Corey?"

ANSWER- Well, hmm ... let's see. He hasn't been in the band for three years, and actually we were so thoroughly disgusted with his eating habits (we are all Vegan and he loves hamburgers) that we sent him home packing in the middle of a tour, bloodied and bashed, without any way of getting home from Minnesota, which is where we were at the time. Actually, that is not entirely true. Not only are we Vegan, but we are also very active voters. Okay—you got me. Corey and the rest of us had creative differences, so we asked him to leave. He wasn't too happy about it, but we had to do what we had to do to move forward as a band. We hope him the best and have no hard feelings. Yes, that's right. I used the phrase "creative differences," which is a fancy way musicians say, "I am not giving you any details because it may cause you to spread rumors about it on the Internet and/or make myself or other people involved look stupid."

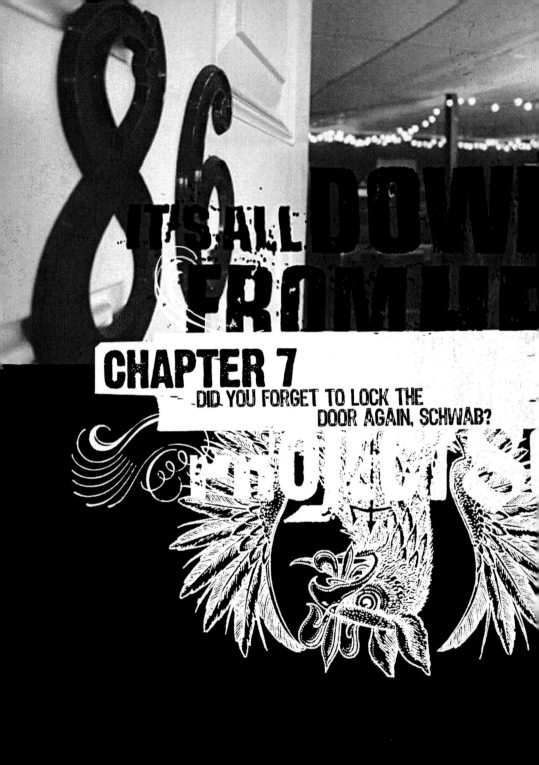

86 IT'S ALL DOWN FROM HERE

CHAPTER 7
DID YOU FORGET TO LOCK THE DOOR AGAIN, SCHWAB?

CHAPTER 7
DID YOU FORGET TO LOCK THE DOOR AGAIN, SCHWAB?

"MAN, YOU GUYTH ARE GREEAAAT. I HAVE HEARD YOU guth. Prothyect Eighty Thix. What do you guyth sooouund like? You guyth play heavy metal, maaaan?"

The drunk guy breathes his vacant phrases right into my face, into my nostrils. I try to inch away from him and dive into another conversation with someone, anyone else. The problem is that there is no one around me who I know I can talk to. So I cannot escape. And so he continues heaving his intoxicated breath into my face.

"What do you play in da group? Do you thiiing? Do you *thiiing?* Maaan, you guyth are coool. (hack) I have been into you foreveth. You play like Korn, like *Korn?* (hack) Maaan, you waaan beer? You waaan beeeer? I know Korn. Korn ith my bros. Korn like my homies. We like thith." He crosses his fingers and pushes his hand into my cheek.

I am usually very patient in these types of situations, but my nerves are wearing thin at the moment. This guy has obviously swindled his way backstage and should not be here. I catch Steve's attention and subtly motion for him to come save me from the belligerent guy. There is something weird about him. Something shady. I really want to get away from him, for some reason, and it isn't just because he is drunk. Then, Steve comes over to me.

"Schwab, we need you over here."

"Okay. Hey, man, take care. Don't drink too much more, okay?" I pat Mr. Faded Guy on the shoulder as I walk away from him.

"MAAAN. Don touch me! Prothyect Eighty Thix!! Prothyect Thix!! Thweeeet. Peeeese!!" He throws up a very mocking peace sign, and then clumsily switches his fingers into a middle finger as I leave him.

It is a beautiful spring day in Fresno, California, 2003. Okay, that's way off. There are no beautiful days in Fresno. Just like there are no beautiful days in the city of El Paso. Fresno is the armpit of California, to say the least. It is usually just a trashy gas stop on the way to San Francisco, but today is different. We are playing a large radio show here, an outdoor festival called "Manfest." The event is sponsored by a couple of radio stations and beer companies, and we have been commissioned by our label (Atlantic) to play this event. Most of the time, these big radio events are pretty fun. There are plenty of fairly large bands (though most of them are beyond cheesy) and plenty of fans present, most of whom have never seen us play live. I love these opportunities, actually. Playing in front of new fans is basically what you should be about if you want your music to be heard. And today there are more than fifteen hundred present. Yet, for all the sponsors on this day, the backstage area is not very secure. Hence, the drunk guy without a pass. These situations are always dangerous because you always have to be watching your gear and your personal belongings. I have heard nightmare stories from other bands about break-ins and suspicious characters showing up to these beer festivals.

Here, today, our RV sits in an area behind the stage that is not fenced in and not heavily patrolled by security. Thus, all the tour buses and vehicles are accessible to the public. This scenario makes all of us nervous, especially our deadly duo of paranoia, Schwab and Alex. Earlier today when we were parking, we both made a comment about keeping an eye out. We have always been lucky in these types of situations, and I am sure today will be no different. Yet, I can't help but feel a little unsettled from my experience with that guy a moment ago. I sense something conniving, even more so than usual ... but I dismiss it as over-analysis and hook back up with my bandmates to take a walk around the festival grounds.

I can't think of an event that I have attended in recent history that attracted such a strange segment of the population. We walk, and when I look to my left, an entire legion of Hell's Angels is approaching, at least two hundred, if not more. They all park their bikes in neat rows right next to the area where all the band vehicles are parked. A comforting thought, to say the least. They sit on their bikes with their, um, "ladies," and drink, smoke, and are merry. Not that there is anything wrong with any of these necessarily ... I am not judging so much as I am expressing discomfort at the fact that there are so many of these dudes so close to all of our gear. We move on. We notice there are different tents and booths set up, each catering to different manifestations of debauchery. Which is all fine, again. I just find it to be, well ... entertaining. You have to laugh when Fresnoians gather. You just have to. It's like attending a class reunion. You don't necessarily fit in with any of the people there, and you probably wouldn't, under normal circumstances, be caught dead there except for the fact that it is too entertaining to miss out on. There is a kissing booth, complete with several snaggle-toothed honeys. There is a big tent where you can sign up for an arm wrestling match—to be held just after our set, might I add. There is even going to be a wet T-shirt contest later. Oh yes, this is a cultural event.

You get the point. Manfest is a phenomenon, a spectacle, a gathering, an awakening. It is so inspiring to see how music can bring us together under the guise of intellectual growth, inspiration, and shared experience. I am proud to be a part of the creative juices that are flowing throughout the audience. The atmosphere is one that exemplifies our struggle, our plight, the human machine, and it is crying out to all creation with art and sound, manifesting its desire for something beyond the confines of this oppressive world. Our minds and souls meld in depth, unity, and conformity to the desires of our Creator. Manfest is the place to be for inspiration and illumination. But don't take my word for it. Just ask the two stoned clowns in full costume, make-up and all, pouring beer on one another and trying to rip each others' clothes off outside the Sumo wrestling circle. Again, welcome to Fresno.

"WOOOHOOO!!" They scream in unison.

Nevertheless, it should be a fun show. I am going to take a nap.

I awake to a familiar sound. Not the tone of the sound, but the melody. There is a band playing a cover song, and the bass is rattling the RV. I am drenched in sweat from forehead to foot, having slept in the top bunk of our sweltering cardboard box on wheels. I am smacking my parched lips together and wiping the sides of my mouth, quickly trying to reenter the waking world. Where? Ah, I know, Fresno. I am behind the stage. Gotta get up quick. Gotta check out the action outside at Manfest.

I clean up quickly and jump out of the RV. It seems I have been sleeping for at least an hour, if not more, and the sun is now beginning to round its way toward the hills in the distance. As

I approach the stage from behind, I realize why that sound is so familiar. Some metal band is covering Portishead's "Sour Times." And it is not a flattering rendition of the song. I get a little closer and see that the band has a set of twins, both playing guitar and attempting to harmonize Beth Gibbons' original tune, with painful results. Steve and I exchange confused glances. Only in Fresno.

Next, a band called "Trapt" takes the stage. The crowd endures a yawn-filled forty minutes of new-school rap-rock (you'd think the kids would catch on by now—we sure did, and it only took us two records) a la Linkin Park. But this is the *GQ* version; Trapt's take on the whole thing is to completely alleviate the tough guy image and replace it with something that more closely resembles Matchbox 20. But they haven't abandoned the attempt at angst, which is a glaring contradiction so hilarious that I have to watch. Sometimes when things are so bad, they are good. Just remember those wise words the next time you are watching a show like *Newlyweds* or *The Real World, San Diego* (by the way, does anyone else think that little girl Cameron is just the sweetest thing on earth? Okay, besides the fact that she is horrendously manipulative, naïve, and has a weird chin. Cameron, if you are reading this, contact my agent, and we can set up a lunch date—despite my former comments, I feel you are young enough that we can work out your rough edges together). Okay, back to the program. So, Trapt closes into their hit single, which actually has been getting really heavy rotation on the radio. It's a song called "Headstrong," but the words talk about how the lead vocalist is so isolated and hurting and so independent in his thinking and so proud of himself for being that way, etc., etc. But the crowd LOVES IT. They go absolutely crazy. They are bouncing and punching each other and running in circles and throwing each other in the air and everyone is taking off their clothes and beer is flying everywhere. You would have thought Elvis had just arrived. No kidding. The power of FM radio, friends. You really only need one song, I guess. It's the magic formula to driving them all crazy.

So, Trapt exit the stage and walk right past the four of us. We watch them act like complete snobs to just about everyone who they come into contact with, and we are laughing to ourselves at them. It's not like they just rocked Wembley Stadium or something. They just played the most mediocre of shows, devoid of anything genuine and completely lacking any honest emotion. That's not to say we are the best band on the planet or anything, but hey, I know what I like and what I don't like and why my taste is that way, and I am not afraid to be honest about it. At any rate, one of the guys is standing next to me, toweling off and having some water, so I decide to encourage him by at least telling him they had a good show. It's not empty flattery. I am just being human, man-to-man, band-to-band. I may not agree with everything they are doing, but I am not going to be a completely aloof jerk about it, because I have no right to.

"Good job, man," I say to said Trapt band member. He just looks at me and rolls his eyes, not even responding or saying thanks. So, I tell him again.

"Good show. Have you guys been playing long?" He gives me the same response, no eye contact, no courtesy. I am starting to have fun with this because I have no idea why he is being this way, especially since I am genuinely trying to be nice. So, I ask him for an autograph. I tap him on the shoulder and hand him a sharpie and a piece of paper out of my pocket.

"Can I have a signature really quick? I don't mean to bug you."

"If you don't leave me alone, I am calling security. Where is your pass? You don't belong back here." Now, I can see there is some confusion going on here, and I don't dare spoil the moment by telling him my band is playing next. This is just too much fun, so I have to take it as far as I can. And for the record, though you may think I am 100 percent malicious, it is not like that at all. I just like having fun in these situations, just to get people to loosen up a bit. Talk about glaring contradictions. Me. Getting others to loosen up.

"Sorry, sir, I didn't mean to offend you. I just saw your band play. I will leave you alone to do ... whatever it is you are doing. Please don't call security. Oh, make sure you watch the next band—they are my favorite." He turns away from me again, and we do not speak. We are to play in about ten minutes. I am about ready to head back to the RV to grab a few things for the show, when I bump into a familiar face.

"HAAAAY. PROTHYECT! MAAAN! I THAW YOU GUYTH IN BAKERTHFIELD IN TWO YEARTH AGO!! MAAAAN. WHEN YOU GOIN' ON?!"

"Right now," I respond. "Are you going to be out there?"

"RIGHT NOW?! OH NO, YOU GUYTH ARE HAARD?! YOU GUYTH ARE HAARD!!" This guy is creepy. Reeel creeepy. I don't know what it is about him, but I really don't have time to talk right now, so I say goodbye, and he throws me another peace sign/middle finger.

I head back to the RV, change, grab a couple of waters, and head for the stage. This is the part I love. I always tell my band to start playing, and I will be out there just before my first singing part starts, and they always think I am going to be late or fall asleep or forget or something. I have never once been late getting to the stage, yet almost every time we have played a show for the past six years, they have freaked out, thinking I am not going to be onstage. I have fun with it. It makes me laugh watching them squirm. I know, I am a jerk. But it's really funny. Trust me.

After our first couple of songs, "Me Against Me" and "S.M.C.," we take a little breather so the boys can tune. This is my time to keep the show rolling and the audience excited by engaging them in a little stage banter. Personally, I hate stage banter, but it is necessary, especially when you are dealing with a crowd that is primarily people who have never seen you before. So I start in.

"We would like to say thanks to all the fine bands that we have shared the stage with thus far, but let's hear it once for Trapt." The crowd, of course, goes crazy for about fifteen seconds. As they are applauding, I look to my right and hunt down that one guy I asked for the autograph with my eyes. When I spot him, he is looking right back at me, smiling and shaking his head. I smile back and wink. I made my point to him. He gets it. I am feeling clever, and I am now having fun at the amazing Brofest.

Next we decide to light into "Hollow Again," which is the song that all of the local radio stations have been spinning something like twenty-seven times a day. As soon as Randy strums the opening chords, a change comes over the crowd. I can feel it, even though my eyes are closed and I can't hear much besides the guitar. Then the heavy part kicks in, I open my eyes, and there is an explosion of flailing fists, fingernails, and flying objects. I have never seen anything like it at one of our shows before or since. I mean, shoes, undergarments, beverages, dead squirrels, and hair extensions all come shooting at me onstage as if shot from a white-trash canon. Then, all the male members of the audience jump in the air and push forward. The barricade collapses and buckles like a pie tin, and here I am witnessing all of this, much more entertained than the audience could ever be.

See, this is how it works: You all think that when you go to a show, the band is entertaining you. That is the illusion we create. The reality is that all the lights and show is just to get you to let your guard down so *we* can be entertained by *you.* You would be amazed at how much people let go at a rock show. Believe me, we have endless video of crowd shots that, if we so desired, would be amazing blackmail material. Kids lose their minds. It is hilarious.

So the barricade is broken, the kids are flooding through, the security is beyond upset (why wouldn't they be? If you were a security guard, wouldn't you be a little peeved?), heads are being stomped on, and children flying from the "mosh pit" like Kermit the Frog being hurdled from a catapult. And I am feeling fine. Now it's time to incite the audience even further.

"Come closer everyone! Closer! I want you to TOUCH US!!" I exclaim with glee in between verses. I am about to launch into the chorus and dive into the crowd for the sing-along. The set-up, the build, the crescendo, and, *and*, AND, **AND** ... NOOOO!! The ultimate anticlimax of all anticlimaxes—I am grabbed from behind, and the band stops playing.

I am now sitting on the stage floor, pouting behind the promoter, who is about to address the violently disappointed crowd. You wait a lifetime for moments like these, then some promoter steals the magic carpet out from under you. I put my face in my lap and sulk.

"WE NEED EVERYONE TO SETTLE DOWN. WE DON'T WANT ANYONE GETTING HURT. NO MORE RUSHING THE STAGE OR CRASHING THE BARRICADE. IF IT FALLS AGAIN, WE WILL HAVE TO SHUT THE BAND DOWN. THAT IS ALL. THIS IS YOUR ONLY WARNING."

He then turns to me and apologizes. I don't say anything back. I am tingling with foul energy. He tells me to help them keep the crowd under control, and I reluctantly acquiesce. No problem. No problem at all. We launch back into our song, the crowd sings along, everyone has a great time, and the promoter is pleased. We finish our set and feel satisfied. I am actually very, very surprised at the warm reception here in good ol' Fresno. I will never say another bad thing about this town ever again. The show was amazing, and we have that unreal emptied/fulfilled feeling that only comes after a really good show. The promoter congratulates me as I head off the stage, going off for what seems to be an eternity about how they want us to come back to Fresno. I tell him no problem at all. Anytime. And I mean it. Then, I talk to a few more radio people just before heading through the flimsy back gate to the RV. I am riding the wave, feeling completely satisfied and one with the universe. Nothing can disturb my great mood at this moment. Nothing at all. Nothing, that is, until I return to the RV ...

I pull out my key to open the door, but it is unlocked. Oh no. Did I leave it unlocked, or did someone break in? I know no one else from the band or crew beat me back here. Paul is still at the board, and Logan is at the booth. So was it me? It had to have been. Yeah, I was in such a rush to get out to the stage that I forgot to lock it. I open the door and go inside to clean up, but something isn't right. Didn't I leave my cell phone on the table? I could have sworn I did. I look around the RV, and almost everything seems to be in place. Everything except my wallet, that is. It has been moved. Or has it? I wasn't paying that much attention in my rush before our set. I grab it and open it. Empty. My heart sinks. There was more than three hundred dollars in there. Three hundred dollars! And to the struggling artist that I am, that is a fortune. I look around for my phone under the cushions on the couch, up on the bunk where we keep our luggage, and on the front console. Nothing. Nowhere to be found. I check my backpack. Nope. I fall on the couch, my palms on my forehead. How could I have been so stupid?! I left the door open at the worst possible show! How?!

Then, I feel the frustration building in me. Who could have done this? Why would you rip off a band, when they are fighting so hard to survive out here? I had been saving my per diems the entire time we had been on the road. Eating less every day, cutting corners, trying my very best to come home with as much as possible. How could I do this to myself? The anger builds, mostly at me, myself, I. I can't help calling to mind my own words through the haze of my swirling emotion: ... *Grabbed hold my enemy's neck and choked 'til he ceased. Blistered with disbelief, I awoke dead. And when I awoke, I couldn't believe it was me. All the time it was me.* What should I do? How am I going to get the cash back? And what about my phone? All my numbers, all my contacts, everything is gone. I put my face in my lap, completely defeated. Just then an idea flashes across my mind's eye. I pull my head up and jump to the console.

There is one chance, and one chance only to get it back. I grab Alex's phone from the console and dial my number. It rings once. It rings twice. Three. Four. Fi—

"Hello," the strange voice answers. I already sense the defiance in that voice. "Yeah, I am looking for Andrew, is he around?"

"I am sorry, you have the wrong number."

"No, I know this is Andrew's phone. Who is this?" I ask.

"Who is *this*?" the defiant male voice retorts. "This phone doesn't belong to Andrew anymore. Now it belongs to me."

"Wow, that's not cool, man." I am trying the gentle approach here first, so I don't scare him into hanging up on me; I am only going to get one chance at this, so I have to be crafty. The guy sounds like he is a little buzzed, so maybe that will play into my hands. I walk outside the RV, trying to keep him on the line as long as possible. I quickly begin scouring the festival grounds, looking for a shady character with a cell phone while I talk. "I am friends with Andrew, and that's just not right to take his phone from him. How would you feel if someone took your phone?"

"I wouldn't care. So who are h--- are you?" he says to me.

I am glancing around backstage and everywhere within eyeshot. I see no one, but I hear the crowd on the other line in the background. Someone sounds off a foghorn nearby in the crowd, and I hear it close in the receiver on Alex's phone. This guy is close. I just have to keep him on a little longer.

"So what did you think of Project 86?" I ask him.

"What?" he says. "What do you care?"

"Did you like them?"

"Yeah, they rule. They are the best band here by far."

Got him. I know right now that I am going to find this guy. Oh yeah.

"Well, this is the lead vocalist, and you have my phone, pal."

Silence on the other end for about five seconds.

"Andrew? Oh no. Is that really you? You guys rule! I loved your band, you guys ... oh, man, Andrew. Listen! I didn't take it, man, honest! You have to believe me." At this point I don't care who took it or why, but I really need to get that money back.

"Where are you? Come backstage where we can talk. I won't turn you in if you can show me who took it."

"Okay, man. You guys are so good, man. I will show you who did it."

"I am standing by the back gate, my friend. Stay on the line until you get to me," I say. Then, I see a shaved-headed guy in wife beater coming toward me. He hangs up the phone as I wave toward him. I am not thinking about anything right now. I am not relieved yet. I am too focused on not scaring away the other "friend" of mine that I am after. He hands me my cell phone, and I take it without a thank you.

"Here's the deal," I say in a low voice into his ear. "You show me who he is very discreetly, and I will make sure you don't go to jail. Do we have a deal?" His eyebrows rise, terrified. I think he knows I am serious.

"Yeah. We have a deal. Don't look now, but he is the tall guy over there wearing the white T-shirt."

"No way, are you sure?" I ask. He nods in agreement. I can't believe it. It's the same guy from before, the creepy one, the drunk one. I tell the guy in the wife beater to disappear, and then I find the promoter, who is standing around socializing backstage.

"Hey, man, I need a favor," I say, once again trying not to look obvious to the guy who stole my stuff. "Don't look now, but there is a creepy, tall drunk guy over there who has no business being backstage. He broke into our RV and stole some stuff of mine while we were onstage. I need you to distract him while I go find the cops."

"Are you sure, Andrew? That is crazy! I am so sorry, man!"

"Don't worry about that, I just don't want him to escape."

"Okay, I will take care of it."

The next thing I do is quickly run over to Alex and fill him in on the situation, telling him to keep an eye on the guy in case he tries to run. He agrees, and walks over to the general area that the guy is standing. I think we have the situation under control and all the players in place for me to get this guy and my cash. I am just about to take off to find the cops when I look back one last time to our boy, who catches my eye as I am walking away. He then looks around him, sees Alex standing near him, and then takes off running!

He hops the fence that leads into the crowd, and Alex is right behind him. I, the champion sprinter and hurdler that I am, take off as well and catch right up to Alex. The whole backstage watches me take off like a rocket. Man, I didn't know that I can move this fast!

The fence is right in front of me, and I promise that I clear the thing, which stands over three feet high, by at least two feet. No way I am letting him get away.

It is in between bands right now, so the entire crowd fixes their attention on this drunk guy, Alex, myself, and our chase. I see him up ahead, and I am fuming. Who does this guy think he is? When I catch him I am going to ...

He ducks behind a couple of trees, and I hear my name buzzing by my ear as I weave in and out of stationary bodies like a speeder bike to follow him. This guy is faster than he looks. Alex and I are neck and neck on his tail, not more than twenty feet behind him.

Then, like a gift from above, the guy barrels into a couple of kids who aren't paying attention and comes to a tumbling halt at the feet of two police officers. Yes. I can feel the blood pumping in my ears. Man, I hope the cops help me this time instead of handcuffing me. Stranger things have happened.

I come to screeching halt with the drunk guy between myself and the police officers, and I tell them what happened. They look at the guy and realize he is intoxicated in about two-point-five seconds, then take him by the arm and lead him out of the crowd as we follow. Of course, there are at least one hundred kids who follow us, creating a circle around the excitement. Did I even need to tell you that last detail? Wouldn't YOU follow if you were at this show? I am sure you would. At any rate, I now have an audience for our little interrogation, so I will be held accountable for my actions. This is probably a good thing because (I won't lie) I really want to go crazy on this guy. No, seriously. I am considering putting his head in a vice, Joe Pesci style. Then I am going to use a plastic butter knife to saw off his ears. Then I am going to pour vinegar in his eyes. I can feel my chest pumping up and down as I watch him intently, measuring him for the kill. Nobody does that to me. No one.

Then I hear that same voice in my head ... you know, the one that reminds you of all the shady, dishonest things in you own heart? No, not now. Go away. I don't need to hear any of that right now. I seriously just want to let my anger well up in me. I want to bathe in it.

No.

That voice keeps reminding me that I am no better. That mercy triumphs over judgment.

"Did you take his money?" one cop asks the guy.

"Nah, bro, I no. Nah (hack). I don know wha you talkin' 'bout."

I interject. "You know you took it, man, c'mon. Officer, you will find three hundred dollars on him if you search him," I say, all worked up. And they do, sure enough.

"Do you want to explain this, my friend?" the officer asks him, obviously not ready to believe much that he says, thank God.

"Thas maaa cash, ma mom gave that to me today. HAY, PROJYECT!! You guyth are rad!! No, I dinin't take it, sir."

"Just admit you took it, and I won't press charges," I say to him, heated, about six inches from his nose. I can feel everyone's eyes on me, waiting for what I am going to do next.

"Nah, I wouldn't do tha to you," he says.

"If you don't admit it, I will press charges for sure, and you don't want that." I am starting to cool down because I feel the warmth of all the people watching me. I don't want to come off too crazy here. Settle, Schwab, settle. In fact, I am glad this is in public, for certain.

"Look maaan. I'm drunk, okay? I don' 'member. Honess. I don'. And I godda warran' out for ma arress. Don' press charges, maaan," he leans in to say this last, as if he thinks the cops can't hear him. I honestly can't help but feel bad for the guy, at the moment, if that were possible.

"Just admit what you did. It's okay," I say, one last time.

"Okay, it was me."

He reaches into his pocket and hands me the money, and the crowd around us begins clapping and cheering. Some of the kids are shouting advice on what the cops should do this guy, from throwing him in jail to feeding him to police dogs. I put my finger to my mouth to shush everyone and to let them know that they should not be so quick to become the angry mob. The cops cuff him and stuff him, then return to me to talk.

"So what do you want to do? You can press charges for sure, if you want to," one officer says to me.

"Nah. He is already in trouble. I am just happy to get my stuff back."

"Okay. We'll deal with him from here."

"Thanks for your help, Officer."

As I walk back to behind the stage, a large herd of Manfestites accompany me and ask me about the whole deal, why I let him off so easy, etc. I really don't know why I did. I guess anyone else in my shoes would have spit in his face. I guess I just felt like the guy had enough to deal with. As I round the corner to the fenced-in backstage area, I see the guy in the wife beater who had my phone. A thought crosses my mind to sick the cops on him, too, because he was obviously the accomplice. He sees me and looks away, obviously afraid and ashamed. No, I have a better idea. I jog over to our merch booth and grab a T-shirt from Logan. Then I go straight over to the guy.

"Here, I want you to have this, my friend. Thanks for your help in the matter." He is speechless and puts his head down, reluctantly accepting my gift.

"I want you to know I know it was you. You broke my heart." Then I grab his cheeks and kiss him on the lips, Michael Corleone style. He pulls away and runs, probably home to his mommy. I think I even saw urine running down his leg as he flew away. All my bandmates are rolling on the ground in laughter, punching the ground and roaring.

Just then Logan comes running up to me, obviously mad.

"What are you doing, Schwab?! Are you crazy? You gave that guy a T-shirt? I am gonna kill him. Just say the word, and I can find out where his family sleeps." Logan is legitimately nuts, and I would bet on the fact that he would enjoy any opportunity he was given to maim someone. If I had a hit mission, he would be the first one I would hire.

"No, man, I don't want that. He learned his lesson, as did the other guy. Burning coals."

"Burning coals?"

"Yeah, there's a verse in the Bible that talks about heaping burning coals on an enemy's head by loving them. It's like leaving judgment up to the One who is supposed to do it, rather than putting it in my hands."

"I don't know, man, I could just set him on fire for you and get it done a lot faster."

"Yeah, you could, but then you would be the one going away in the cop car. I wouldn't want that. Then we would have to find a new merch guy, and that's just way too much inconvenience for us." I laugh and put my arm around him to lead him back to his duties.

We pack up our stuff and get ready to leave, just as they are starting the wet T-shirt contest. Logan asks—no begs—us to stay a few minutes longer, and we begrudgingly decline his offer to watch the hometown honeys get sopping and sudsy. (I know that it's hard to believe we said no, considering we are males, but come on. We have to stick to our standards here. And yes, of course, not to mention the fact that IT'S WRONG.) I see the whole crowd gather around the stage as the girls come parading up, hooting and shouting out intelligent commentary. I hear one guy shout out something that I won't soon forget, and I think it may even be the quote of the day:

"HEY, LADIES, WOULD YOU ALL LIKE TO SHAVE MY BACK AFTER THE CONTEST?!"

I love Fresno. I want to move here.

CHAPTER 8
BAND CREW GONE BAD
PART II

CHAPTER 8
BAND CREW GONE BAD, PART II
THE DEADLY TREE STUMP

IDLE HANDS ARE THE DEVIL'S PLAYTHINGS. DO YOU understand what that phrase means? It means when there is nothing for restless hands to occupy themselves with, bad things happen. It means that when you are bored, you start looking for little mud puddles to rub your hands in. But most of all, it means that when Project 86, Logan, and company have a few days off in the same town, there is bound to be some kind of trouble brewing. And nowhere is this more evident than tonight, in Boston.

I have the worst cold in recorded Schwab history. I felt it coming on a couple of days ago, and as soon as I did, I knew I was doomed. See, when you are at home in a steady climate, it is possible to fight an oncoming cold. You can load up on vitamins, herbs, tea, liquids, and every other immune-boosting agent for a fighting chance at averting sickness. Many times, at least for me, I can start coming down with something when I am at home and never actually get sick because I am guaranteed rest and relaxation. But not out here. When you start coming down with something on the road, you are basically done for. There are shows almost every day, during which you sweat and dehydrate your body to the nth degree, followed by loading out into frigid climates with sweat still gleaming on your skin. Then, you share germs with your entire band and crew on the way to a hotel filled with even more stale, recycled air. Not to mention the fact that you shake hands with about seven thousand people every day, multiplying your germ intake by a factor of millions. It is pretty much impossible to stay healthy out here unless you quarantine yourself the entire time. And that will never happen if you are both the lead vocalist and spokesman for your group. Like me. Add the psychological trauma and stress that is unique to my psyche (self-inflicted, of course), and I am pretty much guaranteed to get sick an average of two times per six-week tour. Now, when a bass player gets sick, he can still play. He will sniffle, complain, hack, and moan throughout the entire process from sickness to health, but the show will go on nonetheless. It is the same with everyone else in the band. Everyone, that is, except for the singer. The curse of the lead vocalist is the fact that his instrument is his body. And the human voice does not work properly when it is deprived of sleep, proper food intake, or mild temperatures. But, the human voice actually *shuts down* when the body is suffering from illness. In my situation, it is even worse, because of the amount of strain I put on my voice due to the style of our music. Yeah, you got it; tour is very hard for someone in my circumstance. Taking care of myself and my health is the most important thing in the known universe when we tour. My band hates me for it, because I am the first one to turn on the heat everywhere we go. I am also the first one to insist on getting my allotted eight hours of sleep, even when we have to drive through the night. And I am the one who will avoid loading out into the bitter cold when I am still sweating. I know it all paints this picture of a whiny prima donna, but I don't care in the least. I know myself, and I know that if I get sick, it will cost us cancelled shows. It's really a no-win situation. I can either frustrate my band by being this way, or cost them shows and income by causing missed performances. The result: much tension in the ranks always.

So, right now, I am devastated by the whole works: massive amounts of green phlegm in my head and throat, a painful cough, and a pulsing body ache. I went to the doctor today, which is a huge chore when you are in a strange town, and he told me to cancel three shows. He said that if I don't, I will damage my voice. I didn't want to listen, so I took ten thousand different meds in the hope that I would be able to sing later in the day. But when I tried to warm up my voice, the result was croaks and wheezing. No way I could even fake it tonight. We had to cancel, so we did. And my band hates me. And our manager hates me. And the promoters hate me. And the fans hate me. And I hate me. Why couldn't I have just tried a little harder to protect myself? Probably because I feel guilty about it, because I allow my band to make me feel that way. When I don't load out, it is a little mental check against me. And when I insist on getting sleep, it is another check against me. Keep adding up checks in my band members' minds, and it will be used against me in tiny passive-aggressive ways sometime in the future, resulting in hell on earth for all of us in the form of inner band warfare. You would never see any of this, of course, because it is all very subtle in the way it plays out. That's the unique thing about our band: Everything from the music to our dress to our interpersonal communication is manifested in subtleties. I don't mean to make things sound so dire, because I honestly do care for all of them. I just can't help the fact that right now I feel angry, and so does everyone else because of my situation. Today's forecast is for more cloudy skies and rain, rain, rain.

So we are off tonight and tomorrow, and we have decided to spend those days in Boston for a couple of reasons. First, everyone is craving chowder. That one is easy. And since our driver/drummer must have food immediately at the onset of even the most minute hunger pains, it is pretty much settled right there. But there is added incentive. Katie, a homeless girl we befriended and kidnapped when we were in New York a few nights ago, says we can stay with some friends of hers in Boston (okay, we didn't kidnap her, and she isn't homeless. We knew her from long ago, when she lived in So Cal with us). So it's settled. We are driving there now as I sit in the back of the RV, removed from social contact as we travel in silent animosity. I hope no one pushes our buttons today, because I am not sure how we will react …

Fast forward to the evening. There is a little party at the house we are staying at, which makes my headache worse. I have decided to drown my sorrows in cough syrup and stay in the RV tonight watching movies, writing, and playing *Virtua Tennis*. Human contact is not something I desire at the moment, and I am plenty content with the fact that all band and crew are in the house hanging out far, far away from me. My mood has not sweetened, primarily because it is hard for me to let go of the principles here. I need understanding, yet I feel like I get none. It's not my fault that the rules are different for me because of my role in the band. I guess if I was in their shoes, I would be upset, too. But it's all eerily similar to a marriage—you can choose to work out your problems together, or you can choose to avoid communicating about them. Either way, you will be forced to deal with each other constantly because you share the same living space. That's the thing that eats at me, though; I have no escape from the tension, and I am forced to resolve it in some form. I don't like being forced to do anything. I resist control in any and all forms, and more than most. Do control freaks fear control the most? I don't know. I don't see myself as a control freak. I just see myself as a reactionary, someone who resists and questions the things I see. That's probably a fairly romanticized profile, of course, because how can you ever be objective when you are talking about yourse—

I hear screaming coming from outside the RV, interrupting my self-analysis session. Though my cold medicine is kicking in and I am becoming a little fuzzy, I still put on my jacket and stumble out the door to check out what is going on. When I get to the sidewalk, I see Katie and some guy yelling at each other. Katie is in his face, pointing at him and getting very fierce.

"YOU HAVE NO CLUE, BRO! WHO DO YOU THINK YOU ARE TO COME INTO OUR HOUSE AND START CALLING ME THIS AND THAT?!!" Katie screams. Evidently this guy is not welcome at the party because he just called her a name, which I cannot repeat here.

Katie is the type of person who is commanding and charismatic. She is definitely not afraid to tell you how she feels. In fact, she is pretty intimidating, if not downright tough as nails. She is the ultimate punk rock girl, too. I seriously wouldn't want her to take a swing at me. And if she was in my face, I would definitely back up. She is almost six feet tall, two inches taller than the guy she is currently yelling at. I am standing about ten feet away from them as Logan and Alex stroll up to check on the situation with me. They fill me in on the fact that this guy is very drunk and was popping off to almost everyone at the party, which is the reason he was kicked out. And now Katie is continuing to tell him off right here on the sidewalk when—

WHACK! The guy punches Katie in the face! Her head snaps backward, and for moment, I think she is going to buckle and collapse. She wobbles and regains her balance, stunned and standing there. Then everything just happens so fast that I have no time at all think.

The guy takes off running up the street just before Katie completely gains her senses back. No sooner does he take of running that I see Logan take off after him, followed just behind by a newly energized and frighteningly furious Katie. Alex and I look at each other, pause, and then join the parade, if for no other reason than to keep things from getting too out of hand. I look up ahead and see the guy flipping all of us off and screaming at us that he is going to murder all of us. He is about fifty yards ahead of us, picking up cans and sticks from the side of the road and throwing them at us as we are gaining on him. This goes on for like five minutes and a quarter of a mile, at which point he turns into a yard. It turns out it is his house, and his girlfriend has just showed up to join our little private party. All I know is that all of this does not look good.

He runs up to his porch where he continues to scream absurdities our way. He says he is going to wait until we are all sleeping and then come slit our throats. He claims he has ties in a crazy satanic mercenary cult or something, to which we respond with laughter. His girlfriend is holding him back in the most cliché fashion, as if her efforts are the only thing keeping him from rushing us. Then Katie approaches the two and gets up close and personal with the girlfriend, as they begin to taunt each other. It is a big mess of threats and finger pointing, as the three of them push back and forth on the porch, twisting and dancing in pre-brawl greetings. I am so entertained by the spectacle that I almost forget how amazingly angry I am that this guy hit my friend, a girl.

But, of course, Logan hasn't forgotten his feelings on the matter for a second, and he has now entered the yard, where there is a large tree stump sitting at the end of the front walk. He looks over at me as he bends to try to lift the stump. Now you have to dig this. The stump is like three feet across and two feet thick, weighing probably a hundred pounds. What is he doing? He actually gets it off the ground and lunges forward, swaying and tripping under the massive weight of this hunk of wood. What is he going to with it? I look over at Alex, and his eyes are huge. We don't know whether to laugh, to follow, to stop him, or to stand here and watch. Then, Logan, tree stump and all, mounts the steps of the front porch, where Katie, the dude, and his girlfriend are all arguing.

"OH NO, Logan, STOP!!!" I yell, realizing what he's up to. Somehow is his flawed mind, he thinks he is going to be able crush the guy with the stump. Talk about delusions of grandeur … maybe he thinks he's a caveman. He lumbers to the top of the steps, struggling and pausing on every step. He lifts with all his might to try to get it over his head, but fails miserably. The result is something so ineffective, so non-threatening, so clumsy and devoid of violence that the image will stick in my brain forever. Instead of hitting our new friend with the stump, it rolls out of Logan's arms, barely grazing the guy's shoulder, then it careens off the porch floor to the ground eight feet below. It is, in fact, the most pathetic display of attempted assault with a deadly weapon I have ever seen.

Offended and furious (though I don't know why—like I said, the whole thing has escalated into hilarity), our female pounding boy then lunges at Logan in an attempt to grab him. Logan dodges, then hops down to the front lawn again, as the guy approaches. Then the guy suddenly stops five feet away from him.

"You know what? I am sorry, man. You guys are right. I shouldn't have hit your friend. Here. Truce," he says to Logan. He is calm, suddenly, and now he is extending his hand to Logan. Logan is just standing there, motionless, suspicious, as he should be. And I am thinking that this guy is truly out of his mind, and I would not trust him as far as Logan can carry a tree stump. But then, true to form, Logan extends his arm to shake his hand. And, like clockwork, the dude pulls his hand away at the last minute and socks Logan in the face.

BAM! He connects with Logan's ear and sends him reeling, but only for a split second, which is the time it takes for Logan's temper to kick in with full force. Our merch guy bounces forward with a kick to the dude's chest, causing him to stumble backward. Alex and I continue to just stand there, not knowing what to do. The next thing we know, Logan has the guy in a headlock, and he is rubbing his face on the fence that lines the yard. The guy is screaming about murdering all of us while he struggles to get free of Logan's grip. He twists, turns, spins, then swings at Logan once more, grazing his face. It is at this point that Alex and I decide to defend our friends. I mean, enough is enough already. The sight of this moron attacking two of my friends in one night is too much for me to bear. Something snaps in my insides, and the next thing I know—

WHACK!! I spring forward and sock the guy in the face, just once to let him know that his little spree is about to end. Then, Alex repeats along with me. BAM! And now the guy is on the ground, and Logan starts kicking him. I am half tempted to join in, but then reality begins to invade my head. Man. Just when this was getting interesting. But I know what is right and wrong here, as does Alex. We are beating this guy up, and I am almost enjoying it, but I know better. Then, I turn around and look behind me just in time to see his girlfriend running to her car.

"I am calling the cops!" she is yelling, over and over again. She grabs her phone out of her purse and begins dialing. Wow. No time to waste here. Logan is still wailing on his victim, continuing to rake his face against the pickets on the fence. I run over to him, the whole world spinning, and try to grab Logan's arm before his fist falls again onto the back of the guy's forehead. I lunge and reach, feeling like I am caught in one of the *Matrix* fight scenes where time slows down so you can see the bullets piercing the air around them. Then, Logan's fist flies up in the air again, this time connecting with—

A shot of numbing pain flies up from my lower jaw, through my tongue, and echoing up into my forehead. For a moment, I am back in real time as the vibration of the hit threatens to tear my skull into pieces. I stagger back, hoping that my feet stay beneath me instead of ending up above me. There are purple and pink blotches blaring in my peripheral vision like neon in Vegas. For a moment, I forget what exactly I was trying to do by running to grab Logan, and my only thought is to pummel the person who just delivered the blow to my jaw. And all of a sudden I can feel my tongue throbbing. I think I bit it when I was punched. I spit and look down to the ground, seeing more red than white. I have my hands on my knees for all of four seconds, looking down at the red in the grass. I look up, and Logan is still swinging away, and I realize that it was he who hit me.

Then I see Alex charging forward to subdue him, and as he does, I reach for my second wind, grab it, and jump forward with Alex to grab Logan. I clench one shoulder as Alex grabs the other, and as we do, our boy breaks free from Logan's grip and tumbles to the ground, holding his head. He is screaming and throwing more ridiculous threats our way, but there is no time left to hang around to see if he has anything left to come after us with. We pull Logan to the street, and Katie follows as we begin running back to the RV. It takes all of seventeen seconds to get there. Must hide. Must pray cops no get us.

I can't believe I did that. I can't believe I hit that guy. I can't believe any of this.

Back at the RV. Alex, Logan, and I hang out for a few minutes in the dark, inside, reflecting on what just happened. I am still so worked up that I am not worried about anything, cops, the guy, or otherwise. We ran so hard back that I am still panting. I know that guy wasn't hurt, and I know we did our best to control the situation, even if it came down to us having to clock him a couple of times to get him to chill. Then I feel my face throbbing and that my tongue is swollen. It hurts, probably much worse than the guy we jacked, who really got off pretty easy. I don't remember seeing anyone get a really hard, straight hit on him. And the blood that was on his head was mild ... small cuts from the fence he was being raked across, no doubt. This is all crazy. I haven't been in a fight since eighth grade.

"Logan, you know you punched me in the face, right? You freaking nailed me!" I say, laughing. He doesn't say anything to me, but just gives me a hug. I'm not mad at him. Incidental contact is not an offense.

"Can you believe that guy?" Alex asks. "I mean, how are you supposed to react when he punches a girl?"

"I have no idea," I say. "All I know is that we are lucky that there wasn't more trouble. You alright, Logan?" He nods. "Cool. Can we go to bed? I am beat."

"Sure," they both agree.

I am just relieved that no one is in the hospital or in jail, including myself. Man, my head hurts. Katie is back in the house, safe, yet still ranting about the punch homeboy gave her, and for good reason. I can hear her yelling and telling everyone inside what happened all the way out here. I climb up to the top bunk, pop some NyQuil, put my earplugs in (yes, I need them to sleep because it is loud outside), and lay my head on the pillow. I cannot wait to wake up tomorrow with a bruised jaw and a scabby tongue. Oh, well, it could be worse, right? Yes, yes, it could.

I feel the conscious world slipping away as sleep is welcomed to my world. Just then, there is a knock at the RV. I am not getting it. I am comfy. I hear Alex get up to answer the door, as I take my earplugs out to hear what is happening. I look through a crack in my bunk curtain to see who is knocking. As the door opens, my heart sinks.

It is two police officers, of course.

"Yes, officers?" Alex greets them.

"Good evening. We received a complaint from a couple up the street saying someone from this party attacked one of them. The only description we got was that he had dark hair and was wearing a 'Zero' sweatshirt. You wouldn't happen to know anyone that fits this description would you?" Of course, it was Logan who was wearing the "Zero" sweatshirt. The very "Zero" sweatshirt that is in plain sight of the cops right now, laying on the counter in the center of the RV. And of course, as if I could have written the script myself, the two officers spot it almost immediately. They push past Alex and into the RV before he can say a word to them. "So, which one of you was wearing this?" Officer number one directs to the whole inside of our camper. Then, Logan pops his head out of the back.

"It was me. I was defending a friend of ours, who was a girl might I add, who was punched in the face by the dude who filed the complaint. Did he mention that when he spoke to you?"

"I am afraid you have to come downtown with us, Son. You can come with us quietly, or we can use force. It's up to you."

Then, Katie sticks her head in the RV.

"HOW CAN YOU ARREST HIM?? HE WAS JUST DEFENDNG ME WHEN THAT FREAK HIT ME! ARE YOU KIDDING ME?!"

"Young lady, you can join him downtown if you want. Now step aside." And the cops lead Logan out the door and off to jail.

That's it. My NyQuil is kicking in. My head falls to the pillow. For the first time in a long time, I realize that I am still very sick. My entire head feels like it's harboring an alien inside of it. I can't believe I am dying in Boston and my friend is being hauled off to jail.

My tongue is throbbing and my body feels like it was used in several random gas chamber experiments during my slumber. I hate NyQuil. I am never taking it again. I rub my eyes, and I realize Logan and Alex are chatting and giggling below my bunk. I pop my dizzy head out the curtain to see what's up.

"Logan, what happened?" I ask.

"Oh nothin' much. I got charged with assault with a deadly weapon, four hundred dollars bail, and a court date which I am not going to."

My eyebrows jump up, and I just stare at him.

"So what was the deadly weapon?" I ask.

"The tree stump, of course."

I bite my bottom lip. Must. Fight. Oncoming. Fit. Of. Laughter. Must. Keep. Straight. Face. Not. Right. To. Laugh. At. Others'. Misfortune. My face explodes with a blast of exhausted emotion and ridicule. I can't help it. Then, Alex and Logan start dying, too. Though none of it is technically funny, none of us can even try to keep from laughing about it. Okay, that's wrong. The whole thing is really funny, and I have no qualms about laughing at the fact that I actually know someone who was charged with assault for attempting to bash someone with a hundred-pound tree stump, which he could barely lift. If the cops knew how stupid this made them look, if they had just seen Logan trying to hit that guy with it and failing so miserably, he never would have even gone to jail.

"Here's the part that's not so funny, though," Logan adds. "Katie came down with Alex this morning to try to talk some sense into the cops, and they wouldn't even listen to her. She tried to tell them that I was just sticking up for her, and she even had a bruise on her face to prove it. They wouldn't even take her statement. They just blew her off because she was a girl. No joke. It was unreal, man. Can you believe it? That freaking guy punches a girl, and I go to jail for it."

"So you aren't going to court on Monday?" I ask. "We will be in Pittsburgh, so we would have to leave you behind. I would recommend going, of course. You'll have a warrant out in

Massachusetts if you don't. But it's completely up to you," I say. "We can't make you go, you know."

"No way I am going."

"Suit yourself. Honestly, I think the whole thing will make a great story, and a tremendous lesson in legal ethics," I reply.

"And how," Logan says. I throw my shoe at him at this last mockery.

Legal Ethics 101 by Logan Shaw, Esq.

Lesson number one: Don't use anything heavier than your own body weight as a deadly weapon in the city of Boston, or you may end up in Jail.

Lesson number two: If you are a girl and get punched in the face in Boston, the police may not listen to your case, no matter how legitimate it is.

Lesson number three: No matter the penalty, you can't just get off scot-free even if you punch a girl in the face, even though the law says you can.

Lesson number four: Sometimes you have to take the law into your own hands, even though you may end up on the receiving end of a felony charge and an uncomfortable night in a cold cell.

And now I raise a reasonable line of questioning: What would YOU do if you were in the same situation? Would you defend your female friend or not? And if so, what would you do? Would you risk getting into legal trouble? Would you be able to lift the tree stump?

Logan told me the other day, exactly one year later, that the guy found him on MySpace.com and offered to visit Logan's home here in sunny Californ-I-A and rearrange his pretty face. And, of course, Logan accepted the invitation wholeheartedly and with glee. And so the saga continues, though I doubt they will ever meet again. I doubt the guy would have the gall. I mean think about it—how much courage does it take to sock a girl?

CHAPTER 9
AND NOW IT'S TIME FOR A SCHWAB LIB

CHAPTER 9

AND NOW IT'S TIME FOR A SCHWAB LIB

I am not famous. This makes me _____ sometimes.
(dark emotion)

Sometimes it makes me so _____ that I want to _____
(dark emotion)   (verb)

people. Like this one time, Randy was _____ing me. I asked him
(verb)

politely to help me clean out the van, but instead of _____ing me,
(verb)

he made this stupid _____ at me. It reminded me of when I
(noun)

would stick my _____ out at my step-mom when I was seven
(body part)

years old. She would yell at me every day for not _____ing my
(verb)

_____, and I would _____ her behind her back as she
(verb)   (verb)

_____ed away.   Except this one time, she saw me doing it while
(verb)

we were _____ing, and she _____ed the _____ out of me in
        (verb)   (verb)   (noun)

front of all my friends. I despised her for this, vowing to become

_____ someday—so _____ that I could _____ her
(adjective)   (adjective)   (verb)

back in front of all of her _____. So today, when Randy made
                            (plural noun)

that _____ at me, I was reminded of the _____ of my
     (noun)   (noun)

youth, and I _____ed him. He just stared at me in shock,
             (verb)

knowing he would never, ever, ever _____ Schwab again.
                                    (verb)

CHAPTER 10
IT'S ALL DOWNHILL FROM HERE

CHAPTER 10
IT'S ALL DOWNHILL FROM HERE

I GUESS MY RANDOM COLLECTION OF TOUR HAPPENINGS wouldn't be complete without a girl story. I mean, rock 'n' roll without girls would be like Carl's, Jr. without the western bacon cheeseburger. It would be like MTV without the pointless reality shows. Like Project 86 minus the Schwab. It just wouldn't be the same. Females (cute ones, that is) can turn a mediocre show into the best night of the whole tour just by showing their faces in the room. Just the thought of those amazing creatures turning up puts a smile on our faces every time (everyone except Steve, of course. He is usually stoic about almost everything except music and his Dutch girlfriend. Okay, well, that's not completely true. Everyone in the band has some sort of serious girlfriend at the time of this writing, except for yours truly). They can be the greatest source of entertainment in a slow town on a slow night when they show up and bring their beautiful magic. When you boil it down, meeting girls is about the most exciting thing about the road, besides playing of course. Although Randy would debate me on that one. He would, for sure, put meeting girls number one and playing number two, that is until very recently, when he landed his new woman.

Nevertheless, my point is this: I would be doing all of you a huge disservice if I did not include something about the subject, since so much time and thought and energy and even lyricism is devoted to the opposite sex in this band. So I decided to include this story, which is my most defining hour, my most influential evening, and my most tragic circumstance. It is the granddaddy of all Schwab stories.

Now, let me explain a few things before I get into this. I want everyone to know (though you won't believe me, of course) that there has never been one single incident of cheating by any member of our band EVER. I know, I know. The cliché about "band guys" is that they are never faithful because they have girls in every single town. And then there is that whole thing about "what happens on the mile stays on the mile," which is a phrase that all touring bands use to describe the tour code of musicians, which is basically an unwritten law. It means that no one in the band or crew tells anyone outside the band and crew what happens on the road. I know what you are thinking. You are thinking it's impossible for us not to cheat. But I tell you, it has never happened, and probably never will. Here again, I guess we are just not the typical band. Now, having convinced you of this, aren't you ridiculously proud of our self-control? Or, do you think we are gay? I guess we all have just realized that cheating is a very pointless activity. Why put all this effort and work into a relationship just to sabotage it with some girl whose name you won't even remember?

Okay. Now there is the little subject of Schwab's singleness. You are thinking to yourself, "How can someone who is as amazing as Andrew not have a girlfriend? I mean, he is great looking, amazingly intelligent, creative, witty, AND the frontman for a moderately successful rock band. ARE YOU KIDDING ME? IF SCHWAB

CAN'T GET A CHICK, THEN WE ARE ALL DOOMED." Don't get me wrong. I have dated many a girl, but they all bore me eventually, hence certain members of my band call me "Short-Term Schwab." And though there are many levels of reasons for my singleness, ranging from genetics to psychology to traumatic experiences to a general skepticism toward the opposite sex, I will sum it all up by saying this: I have never met anyone who I have honestly been into 100 percent. No one. Zero.

No one, that is, except for one girl ...

Her name is Brook Whelan.

We are on our way to play a show in Lawrence, Kansas, at a club called the Bottleneck. It is the summer of 2000. My best friend, James, is road managing for us on this particular tour, a job which he is neither qualified for nor motivated to do. But nevertheless, on this fine evening, he would come through in a way that has never been surpassed by anyone in my entire existence.

A few days prior, James mentioned to me that one of his former coworkers lives in Lawrence and that she was coming to the show with a bunch of her friends. I didn't think much of it. Usually there are guests at every show. It seems that each of us has friends and family scattered across the entire country. Only, I remember that James had spoken of this girl named Brook previously, saying something about the fact that she is "retarded" and "a perfect match" for one of our mutual friends, who happened to be an overachieving attorney with a Porsche and a beautiful home in Newport Beach. So obviously, I would not be too interested in a girl of this type. I am far from an attorney. But then, James starts telling me a few facts about Brook as we load our gear into the Bottleneck.

"Schwab, I don't think you understand. She is the most gorgeous girl I have ever met in real life. She is fun, smart, and has really good style. She's also classy, has a really close-knit family, and shares the same beliefs and values we do. Brook is basically the perfect female specimen inside and out."

"Really? Tell me more," I say.

"Dude, her ex-boyfriend is like some Navy seal guy who is now dating Brook Langton, you know, the girl with the olives in *Swingers*?"

"No kidding."

"Yeah, and she is like friends with Ali Landry or something. This is the caliber of girl we are dealing with here. But don't worry, Schwab, she is out of your league."

"Say no more, my friend."

In retrospect, I don't believe in "leagues." Really, confidence, mystique, class, charm, and all the other things that females find attractive can be learned, taught, trained, and caught. The fact of the matter is if you own it, and you know you own it, and you project that you know you own it without coming off as cocky (which is just a mask for insecurity that most girls can see right through), you are in. My boy James put it best. He said, "Females are the most fierce predators on earth; they can smell fear from miles away." And it's true. If you aren't sure of yourself, she will see right through it, and you will be finished. Trust me.

Of course, I am currently speaking about something that happened years ago, and I had not learned all these lessons yet at the time the Brook event happened. Let me just put it to you this way: I was not prepared for what was coming on this night. No way, no how.

I am backstage at the Bottleneck, hanging out with James and the boys in my band after sound check, when James' cell phone rings. It's his friend Brook. She is outside. He calls me over to him and whispers in my ear.

"Don't tell Randy or the other guys, but myself, you, Brook, and her roommate are going out after the show." I nod in agreement as he walks away, knowing exactly what he is up to and why he wants no one else involved.

Now, there are multiple levels of consideration taking place here. See, my band, at this point in our career, lays very heavy guilt trips on a certain frontman when he appears to be motivated by anything other than the music. Apparently somewhere along the way, we made an agreement that we never wanted to give anyone the impression that we were associated in any way with all the cheesy party bands out there, and focusing on girls, talking to girls, hanging out with girls at shows, or thinking about girls somehow became taboo to, well, primarily Alex and Steve. Never mind the fact that they both have girlfriends and have no personal desire whatsoever to meet new girls.

I, on the other hand, love talking to and meeting new ones, in case I haven't made that clear already. And though 80 percent of our fans are male, occasionally there is a cute little girl in the crowd who catches my eye, who I would definitely enjoy meeting. The only problem is that I get swarmed by dudes every single night after the show, and they all want to talk for hours about lyrics and philosophy and tour stories and on and on. And most times the girl who I would enjoy talking to is eyeing me for over an hour while I am entertaining all the boys, only to leave before I can get to say hello to her. Or she just gets bored with waiting and goes to talk to Randy. Don't get me wrong, I love talking to everyone at shows, but come on here, fellas. Let the ladies come say hello without crowding. There is enough Schwab to go around. And don't take it personally if I talk to a girl before I talk to you, gentlemen. This also in no way indicates that I am shallow or all about orgies or filming porn with them or taking them to the back of the bus. I am just a late-twenties, single male who happens to be in a rock band. The arithmetic should be fairly obvious here.

I get what my band members are talking about, though I find their perspective to be extreme. When I think of bands like Sublime, Crazy Town, Limp Bizkit, or all these other lame bands with chicks in their videos, who obviously write paper-thin songs in an attempt to get frats to make them a part of their weekend revelry ritual, I basically want to vomit bile and tear my own eyeballs out of my sockets simultaneously. We are not one of those bands. We don't have strippers backstage. We don't hire prostitutes. We don't sleep with the Band-Aids or groupies or whatever you silly scene girls call yourselves these days, because we find that to be, well, gross. No way, now how. We write sincere songs about real life and sincere longing for meaning. So yes, Steve and Alex are correct in not wanting us to come off as one of those bands, because we aren't, nor will we ever be. I, for one, have and always been married to our music first and foremost.

But the thing that even the guys in my band don't understand is that the real lyrical quality and honest feelings that so many of the bands that we love possess (i.e. Quicksand, Deftones, Shiner, Portishead, Sunny Day Real Estate, The Cure, and many, many more) so often come from rejection, loss, and longing when it comes to the opposite sex. Failed relationships. Tragedy. It's where all the respectable creativity in the world comes from. This is no secret, and if Steve and Alex had an inkling of a clue, they would be encouraging me to go out and get my heart carved out and served to me on a platter by all the Brook Whelans of the universe. Why? Because I would write some seriously intense songs after the fact …

But back to the matter at hand. My mouth is watering, and I am pacing in our dressing room frantically. I have no idea why. Maybe it's because there has been so much buildup about this Brook girl.

And then that thought—you know, the one you try to push out of your head every single time you meet someone new who might just have potential—that thought announces itself, causing my bowels to churn. *Maybe she is the one.* No. Stop, I tell myself. Don't even think that thought. If you think that thought, she will see it on your face and run for the hills immediately. *But maybe she is the one you have been waiting for your whole life.* STOP. I have to get my mind on something else, like fast. But it's no use. My mind has already started to run, and when my mind starts to run, there is no stopping it. It's like a death train going down a mountain, spiraling log rhythmically to a broken bridge with a bottomless pit beneath it. Self-fulfilling prophecy awaits. Sabotage. Rejection. Nothing left to do but write songs and books about it ... I can see it all happening in my mind before it actually happens. I fall into hopeless, maddening love with this girl, then somehow I make her think that I am retarded, she completely rejects me, and then I torture myself about it for decades to come, living a sordid, sour, miserably lonely existence.

Why in the world am I thinking like this? It's like I have some weird feeling about this girl ...

No. No way in heaven, hell, or anywhere in between I am going to let any of this happen. Here's the new plan: I don't care how hot she is, I am going to ignore her. I am going to ignore her because she and I have no future. I don't care if she is the most amazing person in the whole world. I will not let her know it.

All of this before I have even met this girl. Maybe she has a huge wart on her face. Maybe she's fat now. That's possible, right? I mean, James hasn't seen her for six months, since she moved back to Kansas. Maybe she has been eating huge portions of mama Whelan's down-home Kansas cheese grits for months and has really packed it on. Yes. I find my peace in these thoughts, and convince myself they are fact. I am so good here. Once I convince myself of these things,

I am an oak, a solid pillar of impenetrable defense. She will not own me. She will not make me nervous. She will have no affect on me whatsoever. Why? Because I am NOT going to allow myself to be attracted to her.

This, all before I even shake her hand and lay eyes on her for the first time.

Okay. I get my bearings and begin walking down the steps to exit the dressing room and meet Brook and her friends. I turn the corner into the main room at the club and see James standing with a whole group of girls in the distance. No problem. I will just walk up and put on my best rock god attitude, shake some hands, then coldly walk away, letting all of them know that I am unattainable, out of reach to them. No problem at all. I can do this easily. This is what I do for a living—I channel my emotions for a specific purpose onstage and off. I am an oak …

… That is until I see her blond hair gleaming in the dim light as I approach. She has my favorite hair ever, a bob, which has been my favorite female hairstyle ever since Josie Bissett starred on *Melrose Place* in the early '90s. I continue walking toward them at an accelerated pace, my heart pounding again. Oh no. Not again. Here comes all those terrifying feelings again, but worse. Must. Control. Emotions. Cannot. Let. Her. Know. As I get closer, I get a good look at her face, her color, her shape, and realize a very, very agonizing truth: James did not exaggerate. She is the most beautiful girl I have ever seen, and …

She just made eye contact with me.

I look away casually as I come to standing next to James. There are four girls, including Brook, and several guys along with them. They all cease their conversation as I stand there, projecting a confident air, while my insides are a thumping mass of utter chaos and destruction. Then, James introduces me.

"This is Andrew, everyone. He sings in the band. Andrew, this is Brook, blahblah, whatserface, blehbleh, watchamablah, bluhbluh, and somedude."

Then I touch her hand, and take it in mine. And time stops. And the world spins. And the stars align. And the oceans boil. And the heavens pause.

And I shake her hand like she is a male business acquaintance, make brief eye contact, offer a cordial, cold smile, and turn away to greet the others. But in that brief second of eye contact with her, I scan her from head to toe ... and a cold flash rushes throughout me. *STOP. DON'T LOOK AT HER.* Too late ... I got a great glimpse of her entire frame, and it is now etched in my photographic memory. She is completely perfect from head to toe, and all of a sudden I really feel like stabbing myself in the chest with a rusty blade.

Now, I know what is going to happen here, and it takes all of a millisecond for me to respond to the new thought that has just occurred in my brain: There is no way this girl will like me. Maybe if I was a millionaire and looked like Jared Leto, I MIGHT have a shot. MIGHT. But this girl can get anyone she wants, and there is no way she will show the slightest interest in a moderately good-looking vocalist for a fairly successful underground band. I accept this immediately, and frankly, I am relieved. Very relieved. The pressure is gone. Yes. Yes! As I dwell on these thoughts more, I find myself relaxing, becoming myself again. She will not like me, and that is fine. She is out of my class. Out of my league. Thank God. Now I don't have to worry about it anymore because it is over. I made it through the storm, and I have come out on the other side unscathed. Thank God. There will be no "Brook and Schwab" because I am not even going to go there; I am not going to set myself up for the rejection. I am fine, now, aren't I?

Fast forward to the show. We play in front of about two hundred
kids, which is not a huge crowd, but respectable nonetheless. We
play well, I think, though I am not sure. One thing I have always
been able to count on is the fact that no matter what is happening
in my life off the stage, when I am on it, it is just myself and the
music. There is nothing else for me when I am there, in that place,
performing. But, tonight something strange is happening to me,
something I can't control, no matter how I hard I fight it.

I am forgetting parts of songs, feeling anxious, and I find myself
using every bit of strength to avoid looking to the rear of the room,
where through the haze and lights I can make out the shape of a
certain young lady whom I have now concluded is my personal
antichrist. I am feeling the weight of eyes on me, which is a foreign
concept every other night than tonight. Usually, I am alone,
confident, secure, focused in my emotions. Right now, I feel weak
and powerless. I feel like I am naked.

Then, Steve's bass rig explodes in the middle of the show, and we
have to take a break in order for him to get a replacement. At this, I
rush backstage, completely excited to get out of eyeshot of the crowd.
We must look like fools right now. She must think I am retarded. I
don't even want to play anymore. I want to just sit here and torture
myself. At least back here it is safe and comfortable, at home in the
tragic circle that is my greatest fears. But just as I am getting used to
my self-pity, I hear Steve's bass humming from stage. I guess I have to
go back on, after all. I get up, and somehow drag myself onstage.

Distracted, flustered, and noticeably shaken, I power through the
last five songs of the set. I find that keeping my back to the audience
is a really great method for resisting the temptation to look to the
back of the room. I am on my knees, trying my best to focus, to get
inside my songs again. But all I see in my head is blond bob, perfect
shape, cunning smile. I close my eyes and try to sing my way through

it, and she is there, inside me. Then I open my eyes and look to my left, still with my back to the crowd.

She has made her way to the side of the stage, watching me.

The antichrist is watching me sing.

Somehow I make it through, though my eyes are closed the whole time. It is the only time I can remember doing a show where my mind was somewhere else. I walk off the stage, back to the dressing room yet again, and as I step down, I see her. And I freeze, just for moment. She makes eye contact, and I look away, though as I pass, I catch her scent invading the air surrounding my head. It is the most surreal thing I have ever smelled in my whole pathetic life. A shiver forces its way through me, and the hairs on my neck stand up as I make to the room. Free. At least for the moment.

The next thing I know, James is backstage, hurrying me along to get ready because we are all going out. I tell him I am tired. He tells me to shut my mouth. I tell him I feel sick. He tells me I am an idiot. I tell him I need to load out. He reminds me that I have never loaded out once in my life. I can see that there is no escaping this night. I am being forced to move forward, to head into the wind and face whatever is in front of me. Have I ever been one to cower? I ask myself this, in my head, in all seriousness.

No. I have not. There is hope here. I can do this.

I begin reminding myself of a few things: First, she does not like me, will not like me, cannot like me, should not like me, and I know it. I dwell on this, again. Out of my league. There. Stay there. Don't forget: Schwab does not end up with one like this one. Schwab is an enigma, a lone ranger, an anomaly. Believe it. I feel my emotions swaying with this new meditation. Peace returns very quickly. She does not matter. She does not own me. I have the power to ignore her, the power to relax, the power to let it all go. Schwab can do anything. He can even ignore Brook Whelan.

"Okay, James. I am ready to come hang out," I say.

"Good, because you don't get too many chances to hang out with Brook Whelans. They only come along once in a lifetime, that is, if you are lucky."

I feel my heart dance in my throat as he says this.

I am walking up the street to the bar we are about to hit, alongside James and Brook. I am avoiding eye contact with her altogether, walking behind both of them and carrying myself as one who is above their conversation. She and James are conversing about old work stories and bonding like old friends, while I have absolutely nothing to contribute—which is just the way I want it. I want her to feel like I am the one guy in the whole world that she can't affect. But for some reason that I can't explain, she keeps looking at me while she is talking to James, like I care about what she is talking about. Yet, I can't deny the fact that she seems very polite for trying to include me.

We arrive at the bar/coffee shop and sit down outside with Brook's friends. Everyone is making small talk around me, and I sit there looking bored. A few minutes into it, Brook addresses me, and everyone else falls silent to listen to our parlay.

"So, Andrew. What is it like to play in front of all those people every night? You must feel so great knowing that everyone loves you so much," she says.

"Yeah, it's cool," I say, not knowing where she is going with this. Why is she singling me out? Can't she take a hint? I don't want to talk to her ...

"I'll bet it is. But you are like a rock star! I'll bet you just have to fight the girls off every night you play. You do, don't you?" she asks.

"You know, honestly, it's not really like that for me at all. Most people, especially girls, are usually intimidated and don't even come up to me."

"I find that hard to believe. I would definitely come up to you."

This is pointless. I am getting really uncomfortable sitting here in this circle of strangers, fielding questions, all eyes on me. Awkward, awkward, and more awkward. I can feel my palms sweating and my face blushing with each successive question. Brook must think I am a complete moron, for sure. I can see right through her little sarcastic compliments. But she will not get the best of me. Never. No way. I am not going to be fooled by her flattery. She is just setting me up, toying, playing, probing, so she can find the chink in my armor.

I get up quickly, excusing myself from the conversation, and as I do, I can feel all of their eyes groping me as I exit. I walk to the men's room, and find the mirror. Peering into the glass, I see the face of a terrified little kid who, in second grade, beat up a little girl in his class for not wanting to "go with" him. I splash water on my face and attempt to collect myself. Breathe, Schwab, breathe. You can do this. Just keep ignoring her, and it will all be over soon.

Yeah, keep telling yourself that. You couldn't ignore her if your life depended on it.

Shut up. I don't want to hear it. I will ignore her, and she will get the hint that I am not to be trifled with.

Sure, she will. Don't you know that you are her toy tonight, her little rock star game?

Not if I have anything to do with it.

I have a new plan. I am going to end this night prematurely. I am going to tell James that I have to leave. I am going to go back to the bus. Yeah, that's what I am going to do.

Sure, you are.

I gaze one more time into the mirror, water droplets running down my face like tears. What is happening to me? Here is the great Andrew Schwab, in all his splendor and glory, reduced to a cringing, helpless turd. I shake my head at myself in the mirror. No way I am going out like this. I smack myself in the face and turn to the door.

Don't forget that she would never, ever go for you, Schwab. Remember that when you see her face this time. It will keep you from being affected by her.

As I exit the men's room, I see all of Brook's friends leaving the bar, and immediately I realize that they have to be going home. YES! This is it! The night is over, everyone is tired, and I have made it through the fire! I can retire to the bus with James, unscathed, unscarred, untouched.

But does it go ever this smoothly in Schwab's world?

Nope.

James comes walking up, apparently very excited.

"Schwab! You, Brook, her roommate, and I are heading to a different place, just us four. You are so set, my boy."

"Great." I think I am going to throw up.

"What's wrong? You have been waiting your whole life for this night. Don't blow it because you're scared," James says.

"Me? Scared? Are you kidding?" Because he knows me better than himself, he puts his hand on my forehead in a mock prayer gesture, bowing his head and closing his eyes. I am not in a good-humored state, so I push his hand away before he says "amen." Then he looks at me and just shakes his head in disgust.

"Don't forget you have a responsibility to be my wingman if nothing else," he says. I nod. We begin to leave.

As we walk through the doors, he walks ahead of me with whatsherface, while Brook, right as rain, hangs back with me. Her demeanor is light, fun, easy-going, the life of the party. I am uptight, stiff, and noticeably murky. I wear a scowl, but it doesn't seem to affect her. She takes off her heels and hands them to me to carry. I take them, pausing awkwardly and staring for a moment. She ignores my stare, puts her arm in mine and her head on my shoulder. Then we begin to walk. I am utterly dumbfounded for a second, speechless.

Then, out of the calm dark clouds that always hover above my head, the heavens crack open, and a ray of light falls upon me in the form of a revelation: I get it! It's all so clear now!! How could I have not seen this before?!?!? SHE WANTS TO BE MY *FRIEND*. Of course! Now I can do this. Now I am one with the universe, free and clear.

Free, that is, until she speaks:

"You know, I want to tell you something, but it's kind of embarrassing. So, I am just going to say it: I thought you looked so hot onstage tonight."

My feet stop moving and my heart stops pumping blood, and I think I see my dead grandmother waiting for me at the end of dark tunnel, shining in heavenly light. Brook starts laughing at me. I am not laughing. I am trying to play it cool. It is evidently not working. Here we go again. I am back in the pit of hell, tortured and cast aside. And the antichrist is here with me, stabbing me in the eyeballs with her pitchfork, having a good ol' time at my expense while I burn.

"Thanks," I say. Dumb. I sound like Goon from *Buffalo '66*.

"No really, I do think you are very attractive. I have been waiting all night to get to know you better."

"Well, I think James and I have to leave pretty soon. We have a long drive tonight, and our bus call is in like a half an hour." There. I said it. She looks up at me, slightly disgusted and somewhat annoyed. What, in the name of all that is just and right in the world, does she have to be annoyed about? We don't talk the rest of the way on our three-block walk. She removes her hand from mine and walks ahead of me. I get to the bar, make eye contact with James, who is having what appears to be a terrific time with blahblahface. I walk straight up to him, interrupting, and whisper in his ear.

"We have to leave."

"No. We don't."

"YES. WE DO."

"Schwab, I am the tour manager, and I say we are staying."

I power walk to the bathroom, mad as all anything. I don't look back to see how my "date" is doing. I find the sink, and again splash water on my face, this time smacking myself hard enough to leave marks. I look up to the mirror. I see a broken and tragic figure in the mirror, battered and behind in points. It is as if this is the eighth round of ten, and I am behind on every judges' scorecard by five rounds. There is no coming back unless I knock the antichrist out. My right eye is swollen shut. "Cut me!" I scream at my trainer. He does. Now blood is pouring down my face, and it takes all the wherewithal and courage I can muster to get back into the ring. I still have one more chance to win the match, but my window of opportunity is fading. I turn to the door. Again.

Brook is sitting at a table separate from bluhbluhface and James, by herself. She no longer looks upset. She makes eye contact with me as I approach, and motions for me to sit next to her. I acquiesce, though I sit out of her reach. She scoots her chair over to me, of course. Duh. Why wouldn't she? Then she leans in close to my ear and begins to whisper. But, before the words hit my ears, I am swept with a wave of hellishly mesmerizing scent. It is her smell.

It is Brook Whelan's smell, and it has come to try to destroy me.

I can't even describe it with words, but I know the hair on my neck is standing up, and I am biting down my teeth as hard as I can, clenched. My mouth is dry, and I think I haven't taken a breath in like seventeen seconds or something. That smell, oh that smell. It is a combination of every good, fresh, and clean thing that has ever come into my atmosphere.

I am a dead man.

"Andrew, you seem uptight. You really need to loosen up. You know it's all going to be alright … I won't bite," she says this softly, her breath melting me, turning me into loose clay. Her hands are on my shoulder. Her leg is touching mine. I am just trying not to look at her, again. I am just trying to last, to stay on my feet, to … make it through all this in one piece.

She actually said, "I won't bite." This … to me … the most beautiful girl I have ever seen.

This has never happened in the history of my world. I am beyond shock, terrified beyond all capacity for rational thought. The one time, the only time anyone has ever acted this way toward me … and it is her. She has finished whispering, and now she is just breathing in my ear. She is trying to murder me.

Convinced of this fact, I stand, one more time, prying myself from her grip. I fail. She holds on. I sit back down as she pulls me toward her. She is laughing at me again. I am just trying not to look like an idiot. Just then, like an angel sent from above, James appears at my side. He speaks in my ear.

"I think blehherface wants to leave now. She has to get up early. We should go now." Oh yes. Relief sweeps over my whole frame of reference. I am going to live to see tomorrow. Once and for all, I begin stand up to walk outside …

… But before I do, I feel a warm, soft presence sinking into my jugular. Then, a sharp sting. I stare at James, my abnormally huge eyeballs bulging out of their sockets, frozen in my seat, time ceasing as I know it. He places his hand on his mouth screaming, "OH MY GOSH!" into his hands. I leave my body and elevate above myself, looking down at a scene that would send 99 percent of the heterosexual males on this earth running home to their mommies, sucking their thumbs.

I see, attached to my neck by her teeth, the figure of a girl who has

invaded the core of my being in one fell swoop, one tragic evening. I
see her biting into my neck, capturing me in her web, ensnaring me
for what will surely be all of my living days. I have wanted to have this
girl as my own, as my wife, to bear my children, since before I can
remember. I dreamt of her. She has haunted my dreams. Not Brook
Whelan, per se, but her type, her spirit. She has followed me around
like a phantom since my childhood, and now she has found me, alone
and without my crucifix, my garlic, my silver bullet, my wooden
stake. This was her plan all along: to infect my blood. She, eternal,
creature of the night. Beautiful. Female. Mocking me in laughter,
dangling her very self before me like that carrot I will never reach.

"I won't bite," she said to me.

I knew it was a lie.

And she knows, as do I.

She will never be mine.

*I have heard the mermaids singing, each to each. I do not think that
they will sing for me.*

I return to my body, atrophied, as her teeth exit my skin,
retracting. I do not look at her, but I hear her laughing as the world
spins around me. I don't see the bar, or my best friend, or the people
conversing all around me. What I see is a hazy blend of light, tracing
ember trails, marking this moment in significance. I feel—no ... I
smell—her presence drifting from me, the abating of her aroma, the
fresh, cool scent of petals from a poisonous flower. What is left in her
absence is the dull, ordinary, stale air of hops, beer nuts, and mold
from an ordinary bar in an ordinary town in an ordinary world. I rub
my eyes. She is gone. Outside, waiting to say goodbye.

And so I exit the building, not really sure if any of this is actually
happening. I only know that I have one final chance to drive in the
stake before the sun comes up. She stands in front of a cab, staring
at me. I look past her, around her, down ... pretty much everywhere

but directly at her. Her eyes do not move from mine. I can feel them continuing to measure me. I think I am sucking my thumb, but I am not sure. I can't even feel my legs.

And then she approaches me to say goodbye.

"Brook, it was really nice meeting y—"

I am cut off, my extended hand in offer of a cordial, asexual handshake discarded. She moves toward me, her eyes never leaving mine. She moves inside my safety net, her arms slithering around my waist. My arms hang limp at my sides. She doesn't care that I am not returning her embrace. She moves closer, her legs, her torso, her chest, and everything in between pressing into me, her eyes never leaving mine. All my life, all my days, everything, was coming to this moment, just like you think it will ... you visualize that moment when you will be on the free-throw line with no time left on the clock, the whole world watching, down by one, all the hours of practice and preparation leading up to this one moment. This one moment of a lifetime.

... And she leans toward me, her eyes beginning to close.

... And she pulls me toward her, her hands squeezing the back of my neck.

... And her breath warms my face like a forest fire.

... And she moves in for the kill, the sealing of my fate.

... All of recorded Schwab history hangs in the balance, the apex.

... And what do I do?

I kiss her forehead and say good night.

I kiss her FOREHEAD and say good night.

I kiss her **FOREHEAD** and say good night.

I kiss her **FOREHEAD** and say good night?!?!?!?!?

She opens her eyes, looking up at me with an expression that tells the entire human race the story. It says something to the effect of, "I give up. You win. I am through. You blew it. It's over. You had your shot, and you BLEW IT, ANDREW."

Of course, I don't realize any of this at the moment it happens. I am still in utter shock, operating on autopilot. No thought patterns occur upstairs in Schwabland. He is legally a vegetable. His brain—soup. As she turns from me, I say goodbye, my entire being hoping she turns around one last time to show that she will miss me, my fragile male ego dangling naked, right there on the sidewalk.

She enters the cab, shuts the door, and does not look back.

IT. IS. FINISHED.

As the colors of the normal universe return, and as my heart rate drops back to healthy levels, and as James and I begin walking back to the bus, I am vaguely aware of some lurking horror, some very ugly thing waiting for me very soon, in the very near future. But I am not quite sure what it is. I feel relief, the absence of stress, the decline of pressure. I breathe deeply, trying to make sense of everything that just happened.

"Wow," I utter to James.

"Are you okay, man? You look pale," he says to me.

"I think sooooo—" Then, it hits me all at once.

I fall to my knees on the sidewalk, raising my hands to the sky, screaming, "NOOOOOOOO" at the top of my lungs. Pedestrians turn and look at me from all directions on the street, as I have apparently disturbed their quiet walks with my eternal groans. James rolls on the ground next to me, laughing harder than I have ever seen anyone laugh in all my years. He knows, as do I, now.

I had Brook Whelan in the palm of my hands.

AND I BLEW IT.

I arrive at the bus, and wouldn't you know it—my band isn't even there. I walk to the bathroom, for the third time tonight, to check the mirror. I put down my things, splash water on my face, and stare at myself for the last time on this day. The depth of my affliction, my battle with self, my curse, my fears, my inability to confront my nemesis, is written all over my face. At this moment, I desire nothing but sleep. I look like I have been hit by a train. But then I look closer, and I notice something. I inch my face closer to the mirror to confirm that what I am seeing on my skin is actually there.

There are teeth marks on my neck.

Now, in re-reading all of this and having four years or so to reflect on the events of that fateful evening, I have much to say in retrospect. Of course, I know many of you are wondering if I ever talked to Brook again after that. The answer is "yes." I got her phone number before she left, and I actually got up the nerve to call her once a few days later. As soon as I heard her voice on the other end of the line, I knew that I was dead to her. It was as I suspected before I called her: There are no second chances with the Brook Whelans of the world. Oh, and about those teeth marks: They did not go away for four whole days. And let me make this clear—it was not a hickey. It was puncture wounds. James and I have not spoken to Brook since then, and we are both convinced that she was never actually human. He tried tracking her down several times, and she is a ghost. Perhaps she returned to Neptune, her home planet. If any of you do, in fact, know Brook, please send her my regards and direct her to my website, *www.teethmarksfromwhelan.com*. She can contact me.

Okay, now. That being said, let's make a small list, my class, about lessons that Schwab has learned from all of this, so that all of you may learn at my expense:

1. I will always, always, always be ready for ANYTHING from now on when it comes to "the one." She can come along at any moment,

and when she does, I will be ready. The unfortunate, ironic, sad, pitiful, truth of it all, though, is that they only come around when you aren't looking for them.

2. Though I appear to be the chump in this tragic tale, it is actually Brook who lost out in the end; you and I both know that there is only one Schwab in the world, and there are few who are worthy of him. Again, Brook, if you find me, I will listen to your pleas. Besides, think about how many great songs came out of all this.

3. I currently cling to the thought that Brook has married a professional football player and has several children, one of whom is a son named Andrew, named after the big fish that she allowed to get away.

4. The young lad who plays Andrew in this story has now long since blossomed and is now all growsdup, growsdup. He even has good hair now and knows better than to allow his petty fears to own him. Though, when he plays shows at the Bottleneck in Lawrence, Kansas, he gets a shiver up his spine, if only for a second.

5. Self-fulfilling prophecies are real. Avoid them at all costs.

6. Vampires are real. Avoid them at all costs, too.

7. Though this parable about how gorgeous girls are always attracted to men in the spotlight may serve as a reason for you to start your own band as a means to meet *your* Brook Whelan, don't be fooled. Respectable girls who would make good life companions will normally view rock stars as a temporary fantasy, not legitimate potential mates. We, the insecure, passionate, eternally tragic frontmen of the world represent something that is not real. We, in fact, are not human beings with goals, dreams, and feelings, but we are actually just ornaments, sent from beyond to entertain and give the masses a temporary exit from their mundane realities. We are not real people. That should be obvious after reading this little story.

8. I lied. Number seven is just my sarcastic way of confessing the

fact that though I started this band to try to get chicks, it actually keeps me from meeting cool ones who don't want to use me for some sort of ego stroke.

9. I lied again. Number eight—when I said I started this band to meet chicks, I actually meant that I started this band to *repel* them, so I could eliminate distractions from my "art," which is the only real woman in my life.

10. Last, but not least, I would like you all to know something very important: When I say that I "blew it" in this story, I do not mean that I think I failed because I did not kiss Brook. Though that does, in fact, suck, I actually blew it because I allowed my own twisted emotions to prevent me from being myself. In all things, I believe in all seriousness, you have to be yourself. If something is keeping you from being yourself, you should ask yourself why. Then you should write a book about it for therapy. Then you should go scream at strangers about it across the land, on tour. If this doesn't help, then I suggest you seek professional attention. If you can't bring yourself to seek professional attention because of pride, ego, or the thought of what your peers will think, then refer to the top of this list and reread all of the subsequent points. Repeat as needed, up to four times daily.

11. Happy hunting, boys. Don't settle for someone just because you are lonely. Wait for her. She will come. Unless you screw it up, of course. Wait. I mean, um ... I have most definitely gotten over Brook. No really, I have.

IT'S ALL DOW FROM HE

CHAPTER 11
WHY I DO WHAT I DO

PROJECTS

CHAPTER 11
WHY I DO WHAT I DO

I AM ON MY WAY INTO THE CLUB WITH ABOUT THIRTY seconds between this moment and the first lyric of the first song of our set. It is a cold, rainy evening in Maine, early 2003, and I am jogging from the RV to the venue, across a mostly vacant parking lot. Out of the corner of my eye, I notice two approaching silhouettes, shrouded by the mist, moonlight, and parking lamps. They mean to engage me, no doubt, as I am quickly running out of time. As they emerge from the shadows, I notice it is a teenage boy and his father, wearing downcast expressions. I begin running to get to the venue, trying to get inside before they can cut me off. It's not that I don't want to talk, it's just that, well, I can't exactly leave my band hanging on the stage, now can I?

"Andrew," the teen shouts, increasing his pace to intercept me. I turn to greet them in response. I notice the kid is wearing a very old Project 86 T-shirt.

"How are you guys?" I reply. "Thanks for coming out to the show tonight. Actually, I am about to go onstage, so will I see you inside?"

"Nope. We aren't going to your show. We came here to tell you we can no longer support your band. *Truthless Heroes* is a completely depressing record, and it is really too bad that you guys have left the Christian faith. And we saw you running away from us, which also proves your heart is in the wrong place."

Oh, perfect timing.

"Listen, I honestly would love to talk to you about this, but we are about to start playing any second. Will you please stay and talk to me after the show? I would be glad to answer any questions you may have."

"No. We aren't coming. We can't support you guys. You have let so many people down with this record. We are leaving." With that, the two turn their back on me and head toward their car, as I spin and sprint to the stage. Thus ends another very productive conversation between the artist and fan, promoting a wealth of understanding and relationship. I take the stage to an almost empty room, no more than a hundred in attendance. Needless to say, this night is darkening quickly, along with my mood and focus.

As the months have passed since our third release, *Truthless Heroes*, the perception of our band has sunk by the hour. What was once a roaring inferno of public excitement from *Drawing Black Lines* (our second release, which was a big underground success, selling more than one hundred and ten thousand copies) and into writing this latest release has now become a whimpering flame no larger than a Bic. How do I know this? I guess when you visit the largest record store in Los Angeles and notice that there are more copies of your newest record in the used section than on the actual shelf, you begin to ask questions. I guess when management promises and radio hype taper off into disappointing sales, you begin to get a few answers. And I guess when the label cancels your second single because (and I quote) "The lyrics conflict with the Iraqi war effort," you get a few more answers. What was once a half-million dollar album has now been heralded by a large portion of our fan base as overproduced and void of even a remnant of the raw energy that was present on our previous release. The mist gathers on my forehead as I reflect on all of this, standing before my lukewarm audience as we launch into our first song.

"You were conceived on a storyboard ...in an uptown highriiise!" I scream into the mic with all the emotion I can muster, which actually just feels like a whimpering gasp before the final bucket kick. These lyrics, from a song called "Another Boredom Movement" on our new record, convey the amount of control major record labels have over the music that enters or (in our case) doesn't enter the marketplace. I bask in this truth, as my thoughts are far from here, far from this stage, far from anything positive, bright, sunny, or hopeful. I don't even feel like being here right now. I wish I was home in my bed with a Tylenol PM to guarantee twelve hours of escape.

I remember the conversations we had in our studio about writing this record, how we did not want to be pigeonholed as a Christian band, a nu-metal band, or a hardcore band, for that matter. I recollect arguments over the sound of the record, how we did not want to cater to this market or that market, how we did not want to limit ourselves or our audience. We demoed and demoed and demoed some more for fourteen months, trying to land our dream producer and convince our record label that we were radio friendly, all at the behest of the pressure by all those around us to have a huge, hit record. Executives came by our studio to check our progress and comment on our sound. Managers told us how we needed to play the game. Just play the game ... to succeed. I remember being told that if you do not give the label what they want in terms of commercial material, they will not push your record, and your career will end. I remember being told that we have no future as a band, no meaning, no place in music whatsoever if we did not score a multi-platinum hit. Just play the game ... to succeed.

"Is there anywhere you can run to hide from the thieves?... 'cause eternity's on sale today for a fee ..." I scream during the second song in our set, hoping that I can scream long enough, loud enough, to get it all out. Hoping that at the end of this agonizing hour, my soul will finally be emptied of all its regret, all its second guessing. I look out at the lukewarm audience as a half dozen kids are bumping into each other in their most sincere impression of a real pit.

I recall being told that the only way we will be able to build a worthwhile career is to evolve away from the things that had made *Drawing Black Lines* so successful. I recall storming out of the studio when I was being told to sing, sing, sing, when all I wanted to do was scream, scream, scream until I ached. I recall the feeling of hopelessness I felt every night, coming home from the studio, resenting so deeply that we were being told what to do, how to sound, who to be. I remember debating my band members, wanting them to write heavier songs that I could scream about my trials and tribulations with all the angst of our last record. I remember them responding, saying that we needed to give the label the types of songs they would understand, not just songs our fans would understand. Powerlessness. Subordination. Chains. I recall giving in to anger, subversion, and anxiety as I lie awake, stomach in utter knots, unable to steal more than three hours of sleep. I recall the mix sessions, hearing what were supposed to be the heaviest tunes ever created, now compressed, polished, and squashed until the emotion was glossy and paper-thin. I remember pushing these feelings far, far away, hoping that commercial success would be worth it.

"Remember what it's like to be you ...Remember what it's like to be me? ... all that I see, these eyes in my dreams, these thought police

coming for me ..." I proclaim, somewhere in the middle of our set. I have forgotten why I am here, what I am doing, where I am going. The incrimination of my own words is weighing so heavily upon me that I can't even move on this stage. I am screaming the words, hoping that as they exit my body, I will escape them, that I will escape the disappointment they represent.

I recollect the sheer audacity that was born in me to somehow express in words, even if I was the only one who understood them, how much I hate being told what to write, how to feel. I recall so clearly how I wanted every single word to express my resentment toward everything and everyone that had taken what was pure to me and tried to make it just something to sell. I remember writing in my room, in the quiet hours of the morning, about the fact that this is a witch trial, modern day. I remember playing the victim, giving in to all these voices in defeat and utter submission, hoping that it was I who was wrong all along by clinging to any sort of values or standards or purity.

"We'll eat what's left of you before we're through ..." I belt from my gut as the moments stretch forward, noticing the middle-aged gentleman in the back yawning during our performance. The three girls in the front are making goo-goo eyes at me, just out of eyeshot range of their boyfriends, who are failing miserably to start a pit behind them. They reach up toward me and grab my legs in unison, fawning and groping, making me the object of their giggles. Then, the three laugh uncontrollably as I twist free from their grasp and move to a different part of the stage. I have successfully entertained them. Rather, they have successfully entertained themselves at my expense. I can't say that I care at the moment.

Oh yes, I do remember all that was intended, and all that could have been with our third record, *Truthless Heroes.* I remember sitting in an office high up, downtown Manhattan, with a very powerful record executive as he praised our newest record, playing our single "Your Heroes Are Dead," reveling in its accessibility. I do recall, yes, being able to almost quiet my conscience at that moment, hoping that despite the sinking feeling of compromise and helplessness under the might of this label, this song would make it all worth it. I remember being told by those closest to us that we would go platinum. And I remember almost convincing myself that this is why we were doing this. I remember all of this and more as we play for this empty room of kids, the height of loneliness, knowing that our much-anticipated third record has not and will never achieve any commercial success. Here, six months after its release, I stand at odds with our record label, our manager, and our fans, for giving in, even if it was ever-so-slightly, to what everyone else wanted me to do. And I feel alone, alienated, even by my own bandmates. Here, on this stage, I feel no attachment to what I am doing at this moment. I want out, for good.

And so the set comes to a bitter end, as I try my best to convince everyone in the room that I am so passionately consumed by the performance. I think I may have fooled them. You can fool anyone if you push those little voices inside you far enough down. We lie to ourselves more than we lie others. In fact, it is because we lie to ourselves that we can lie to others. And, oh, have I lied to myself.

There can be no fulfillment in anything without the proper motivation, no matter what we tell ourselves, no matter how much we try to convince everyone around us that the truth is otherwise. And when proper motivation is removed, what is left is pain, guilt, and longing for something pure, something we knew we could have had but weren't courageous enough to achieve. I remember being content with simply inspiring others, offering them hope amid suffering through song and verse. I do recall a time, seemingly ages ago, when I knew what I was doing and why I was doing it. But when your once sturdy foundation is replaced by sand, you can only expect one thing: that it will fall when the fickle wind decides to turn against you and blow. I exit the stage on this very night unfulfilled and filled with remorse, knowing that we have put all of our hopes on an empty whim: record sales, success, dollars and cents, the hype of the passing moment in this industry. We wanted to be the next big thing on *Truthless Heroes*, whereas we were, in the past, content with just being us.

I retreat to tepid applause and a few cat calls to my backstage seclusion. A kid yells, "Bring back to fro!" just as I am leaving sight of the audience. My bandmates and I don't speak. We know that the last two weeks of shows on our current six-week tour have been disheartening. We know that we are not being given the attention we deserve from all the people who are supposed to be working for us. We know that we don't know who we are or where we are going at this point, when it all seemed clear not only a couple months prior. We were all sold on the idea that things were going to take off, but here we are, with the grim reality that nothing ever goes as planned. And we feel alone. And we *are* alone, so it would seem, at this very moment. We are at the very breaking point of our band's existence.

But it is in our moments of isolation that true motivations are revealed ...

But it is only when we have lost everything that we are truly free to see ...

After a few moments of cooling down backstage, I return to the merch booth, hoping that my presence will attract more sales. I put on my best political charm, hoping that my countenance does not reflect how I truly feel. A few kids approach the booth, ask questions, and buy shirts. My three lady friends from the front row approach with their boyfriends, giggling and telling me that we had a good show in a somewhat mocking tone. I reply with a polite "thank you." I rub the sweat form my forehead and let out a huge sigh as they turn to leave, wondering how long it will be until the smooth skin on my forehead turns to wrinkles. You think about such things when you spend five years of your life devoting your time in energy to something that currently seems ultimately doomed to be a waste. It's called stress. Anxiety. Disappointment. These are the things that bald heads, gray hairs, wrinkles, and ulcers are made of. Failed dreams equal heavy weights in our hearts.

I am interrupted from my worrisome thoughts by a lonely, meager kid approaching the table. He looks even more distraught than I feel. He has bad tattoos and huge bags under his eyes, looking as if sleep has been avoiding him for weeks. And as he comes closer, I see that his eyes are red and watery, as if he has been shaken up by something severe. I am curious, and my attention is drawn away from my selfish wallowing, for the time being at least. I make eye contact with him as he speaks to me.

"Is there some way we can talk in private, man? I know this sounds kind of weird, and you guys are busy and all, but I have some important things I would like to talk to you about, Andrew," he says to me.

"Of course we can," I reply. "Follow me, and we can talk about anything you want."

I lead him back behind the merch table and into a back room at the club, away from would-be interruptions. I am a little overwhelmed at his candor, not knowing what to expect when he does decide to speak. I am also hoping that he is sincere in his desire to speak to me about something real, and that he isn't just someone who just wants to get near me because he likes my band. You would be amazed at the stories that people come up with to have an excuse to talk to someone they idolize.

"First of all, I want to tell you how much your music means to me, Andrew. I bought *Drawing Black Lines* a couple of years ago, and it changed my life. I'm not some crazy fan or anything. I'm just someone whose life you have changed. Your lyrics are so passionate and filled with hope, though I can tell you have gone through real pain. It's just … so … real. And that's so rare. I actually feel your hurt when I listen to it, and it makes me long for something real in my own life."

I am currently feeling this guys words, for some strange reason. I mean really *feeling* them. You would think that would be obvious, but when you have the same conversation with so many people so many times, over and over again for days on end, it is impossible to feel a deep connection with every single person who approaches you. But this guy has my attention. I can sense he has deep pain and a very real need for something. And all of a sudden, my petty cares about disappointment and my music career seem very far away.

"Thanks a lot, man. Your words really encourage me. What's your name?" I ask.

"Jeremy," he responds.

"Nice to meet you. So, tell me—what do you really want to talk to me about?"

His face drops, and tears begin to appear in his eyes. He looks embarrassed and tries to wipe them away before they stream down his face. My heart begins to open to him even more as I see this happening, sensing his earnest desire to confess, or share, or something. I can just tell he has something very important to reveal.

"I have to tell you this, only because I have to tell *someone*. I am sorry to put you on the spot like this, because you don't know me. I feel a connection to you because of your music, but only because it speaks so closely to what I am going through right now. Please don't think I am just some weird fan, because I'm not."

"It's okay. Don't worry about it. Just let it out, man. Sometimes just the act of speaking about something heavy on your heart frees you up enough to take steps in a new direction. Trust me, I am here to listen. This is why our band was started in the first place, to inspire those in a low place." I say all of this hoping that I can convey to him how much I truly want him to know that there will be no judgment on my end. God knows I have had my fair share of pain and hurt in my day. This conversation is going somewhere much needed. I can feel it. But who needs to have this talk more, him or me?

"Alright, here goes. I have been strung out on heroin for basically the last eighteen months. I am living on the streets right now, completely homeless. I stole money from my family, and they don't trust me anymore. I have nowhere to turn, nowhere to run. I slept in the park last night. I guess I am telling you all of this because I want you to know that the only thing that has kept me going throughout all of this is your music. If I didn't have it, I would have probably been dead by now." His eyes begin to well up at that last sentence.

Now track with me here. I have basically just been told that I saved someone's life that I don't even know, that I have never seen, that I have never met. I am sure guys like Trent Reznor get this bit all the time, and they are well accustomed to the story, if not even a bit jaded to it. But for a guy in a mid-level band struggling for legitimacy and meaning during a time for us that seems absolutely devoid of anything hopeful or inspiring, this kid's words are a direct injection of life. I am beyond words. My entire world of misaligned priorities has just been completely obliterated. Here I am, so concerned about my album sales and future as a professional musician, while this guy is sleeping under newspapers on a bench.

"Have you tried going to rehab? I have a few friends back home who went through the same thing, and they had great experiences with rehab. There are even some places that will take you in for free, as long as you commit to the program. I know Teen Challenge has that type of program," I say.

"I just don't have any hope that it will help. I feel like there is nothing that will pull me out of this cycle. Have you ever done heroin? If you haven't, there's no way I can explain to you how much it takes a hold of you."

I shake my head. He pulls up his sleeves and shows me his track marks. The veins on both of his arms are black near the elbow joints. I cringe internally, but hide the reaction on my face. If I had any doubts as to whether or not he was the real deal, they just went out the window. I am thoroughly and completely ashamed of myself at this very moment. I have everything. He has nothing. I feel the weight of his spirit, knowing he is completely at the bottom and that I am the last buffer between him and giving up completely. But what can I do? I am in town for one night. I have no chance of playing any role in his life whatsoever because of my lifestyle. All I know is that I need to give him anything and everything I have. The burden is deep, his reality now weighs on me. I feel a strange responsibility for him in my conscience, knowing I do have something for him that he may not get anywhere else. I know immediately what I should say, what I should do, as if it is being decided for me, but not by me. I lead him out to our RV, away from the club and distraction, and invite him into our home on wheels. Though this is a right that few enjoy, if for no other reason than refuge and privacy, I know that opening up my house to him is the least I can do.

"Tell me what you need. Clothes? Blankets? Food? Drink? I can give you anything we have and more." I quickly put together a bag filled with granola bars, soup, a blanket, a sweater, and bottled waters.

"Thanks so much, man. You don't know what this means. This is the most kindness I have been shown in months. Everyone I know has cut me off, and for good reason. I don't deserve another chance."

That's what it all comes down to, doesn't it? Does anyone deserve it? Do I, right now, with all my poor attitudes? Does he, right now, with his dirty blue balloons and thieving? I think every single one of us knows the answer to that one deep down. The answer is no. No, we don't.

"Honestly, Jeremy. I don't have much to give you right now. I mean, I am leaving tonight, and I would take you with me if I could. But I can't. The fact is that our conversation will be a memory in a few hours, and you will be left with the same thing you are left with every day: a decision. The truth is that you already know the answer to your question. You don't deserve a second chance. Neither do I. But if you were given one, would you take it? If you had the chance to put it all behind you, would you?"

"Yes," he says, tears welling up again.

"You have to listen to me right now, because you are at the turning point. If you leave here tonight without hearing my words, continuing down your present course, it won't be long before you lose your life. It doesn't matter how you got where you are now. It doesn't matter the decisions you have made prior to this. What matters is the decision you make right now, and the ones you will make from this point forward. Look, I am going to be more vulnerable with you than I usually am with people who come up to me at shows. I haven't exactly been living the most fulfilling or peaceful existence lately. In fact, I have been depressed for the most part this whole tour. I am just having a hard time finding meaning in anything I do right now. But you coming to me and talking to me has really smacked me in the face. What I am going to tell you may sound crazy, if not completely ridiculous, but I know a way out for you."

"No matter what it is, I want it. I just don't want to be who I have become."

"I want you to know I have tried so many things to try to find some sense of meaning in my life, but I've come up empty on all counts. I mean, I've tried everything. Girls, success, money, partying … it's all the same thing. It's all a quick-fix, an escape mechanism, a temporary treatment of symptoms without acknowledging the actual sickness. And we are all wired the same when it comes down to it. We are all searching for some sense of fulfillment to appease our guilty consciences and make ourselves feel better, in the long run. When you boil it all down, this is the essence of how we spend most of our time. It is all just basically a search to fill the hole, the void. Do you feel it? And the funny thing is, the harder we try to fill the hole, the more destructive we become. It's how humans are built. We have a natural propensity for self-destruction. The more well-adjusted of us can keep it together on the outside, but we still feel that empty spot when we finish our day and lie alone in our beds at night. I don't care who you are. And whether we want to admit it to ourselves or not, we are reaching, stretching toward some meaning in everything we do. Do you understand what I mean?"

"Yeah."

"And I know this sounds crazy, but I have to be honest here. There is only one place I have ever found any sense of truth or peace in my own searching. Maybe you have heard it thousands of times, and chances are you have. But there is something about hitting bottom that forces us to turn to things we wouldn't turn to normally. I am telling you, man, the only place you will find any fulfillment, in my experience, is in God."

At this, I reach in my drawer and hand him my Bible. I only have one, and I have had it for years, complete with notes and personal remarks. I feel so strange saying all of this because I have been so devoid of hope lately, but there is no denying the fact that it must be said right here, right now. It's amazing how these encounters become a wake-up call to the messenger as well as the receiver. I wouldn't rather be anywhere else in the entire world than here at this moment.

"Here. Take this. It has been a light to me, despite what so many in our culture say about the fact that Christianity is outdated and dead. I think the most amazing thing contained in these pages is the fact that forgiveness and cleansing is available for anyone and everyone, if they are willing to turn from their ways and admit that with ourselves at the helm, we will fail. If we are willing to humble ourselves and confess, then He is willing to forgive. Isn't that amazing, once you think about it? It does not matter what we have done."

He nods, silent. Intent and remorseful, his expression says all that needs to be said, adorned with a worn expression that concurs with my last statement. Forgiveness is hard to find. He knows, as do I. Forgiveness is hard to find. And I need it right now as badly as he does.

"Do you think I could be forgiven for what I have done?" he asks me.

"Yes. Without a doubt. We just have to believe in the Son of God. We have to believe that we are forgiven and change our ways. He does not want to see us in the state that we are in. You know, in many ways I am in similar shape as you. Just tonight, onstage, it was almost impossible for me to get the words out because my heart was so heavy with remorse, regret, and hopelessness. This conversation is as needed for me as it is for you. I am truly amazed at how this night is turning out. Do you want to pray together right now, and let it all go?"

"Yes," he says.

And we do. And it is everything that both of us need. We confess together, before heaven, eyes shut, hearts open, not caring what the world around us thinks at that moment. I actually can feel his burden lifting, hope entering his mind, his thoughts. It is a beautiful thing, to say the least. He confesses all he stole, all he injected into his body, and all the ways he indulged in hopeless thinking. I confess all my disobedience, my cynical attitude, my desires to store up success as some sort of end-all-be-all fix to my own insecurities. But most of all, we both confess filling ourselves with utter poison when another answer was offered all along. Then we open our eyes together, and all the world seems to have changed while we were away.

"Do you sense the hope?" I ask him.

"I do," he responds.

"Listen, man. You know I can't stay here with you, or else I would. We can stay in touch after tonight, though. I'll give you my email address. You have to promise me you will contact your family and enroll in a program. Do you have one in mind?"

"Yeah. There's one not far from where I have been staying. I promise I will go there tomorrow. Andrew, you have no idea how much you helped me tonight. I think you may have really saved my life all over again. I don't know how to thank you for talking to me."

"I should be the one thanking you. Your courage and honesty truly convicted me of how much of a coward I have been lately. You have helped me just as much as I helped you. But the reality is that there was a definite reason why you came here tonight. I can see that so obviously it is scary. I have a couple of questions, though. First, how did you get to the show tonight?"

"Oh, I snuck in the back when one of the bands were loading in between sets. I didn't have any money, of course."

A smile creeps over my face. I can't help but think about the kid and his dad before the show, and how people like them would have probably kicked this kid out of the show if they had caught him.

"That's pretty funny," I say. "It's amazing how ironic these situations can be. Okay, here's my second question: Did you have any ideas about the stereotype about our band before tonight?"

"Nope. I just liked the music and felt a real desperate search for hope in it. I guess I always just felt that there was something in it that pushed me towards staying alive. You guys don't seem at all to be like those lame Christian rock bands who are trying to make Jesus cool. You are a real band that plays real music. To be honest, if I had thought that you guys were a Christian rock band, I wouldn't have come tonight. Actually, I didn't even know you guys believed in God at all before tonight."

It is about eighteen hours later. We are about four thousand miles late for an oil change, and we are pulling into a gas station/service center called "Lube Break" or something to that affect. We are all fairly exhausted and quiet, still waking up and slightly groggy. We all sit, for the most part in silence, much akin to the way you would sit and read the newspaper in your own house on a Sunday morning. At this moment, I am calm and hopeful, knowing I am moving forward into purpose, whatever that may be. I look around at all of us in our home on wheels, thankful that we have this RV as a place where we can live on the road. Even if it is not ideal, it is still a home for us, and I am thankful, right now, for all I have been given. I think about Jeremy and his decision to get help, hoping he will keep in touch and let me know how he is doing, hoping that this will all make sense and have a happy ending. I am, here, now, completely basking in the fact that my life does have some meaning and that someone's life was affected by us. I know how easy it is to use a situation like this to make myself feel better, to make it all about me. But I know better. I know that I am pretty empty without the provision of above. As cliché as it sounds, this, again, is the only thing I can find any meaning in.

So you think this is where the story ends, don't you? It would be a perfect, cute little wrap-up to my cute little book of stories with cute little Christian morals, wouldn't it?

Nope.

So, Alex is outside the ve-hic-oh, talking to the mechanic about changing our oil. He has been gone quite a while, so I lift the corner of the blinds to see what the holdup is. I see him engaged, apparently in a fairly in-depth conversation with the guy. There goes Mr. "can't-resist-the-opportunity-to-hear-himself-tell-exaggerated-life-stories-to-strangers" Albert, I think to myself. I am rolling my internal eyeballs, wishing that for once in his life, Alex could move in a gear other than first. We have another show to get to tonight, and as always, we are going to be late if we don't get a move on. But it's cool. I am calm. I am at peace. There is not much on this day that can bring me down, not even Alex's unearthly commitment to resisting punctuality at all costs.

Or so I think.

The door opens and Alex pops his head into the RV. He looks distressed.

"Schwab, can you talk to this guy? He has some questions for you," Alex says.

I don't know how I know, but I just know. Alarm bells are ringing in my head. I see the mechanic behind him, peering over Alex's shoulder with invasive eyes, taking mental notes on the picture he sees on the inside of our RV. I can tell he means to board and have a conversation with us. Then, he pushes past Alex and enters our home, uninvited. I can tell by the look on his face that he has some problem, and he means to unleash it on us. My sixth sense tells me that this guy has somehow been sent by evil forces to steal my newfound P.M.A. from me.

And sure enough, the guy just starts unloading.

"So, you guys are in Project 86, right?" he asks in an accusatory tone.

"Yessir, we are. What can we do for you?" I respond. Everyone in the RV is tense and silent, feeling what I am feeling from this guy. Of course, no one is going to dare help me in this conversation. No way. Confrontation is beyond the capacities of our entire band, yours truly excluded. I am the elected spokesman, so these types of conversations fall into my lap every time. And of course, I can also see that the second Alex was confronted with some awkwardness with this guy, he defaulted to me. Thanks, again, Plow. I owe you another one. Okay. I collect myself within an instant, preparing myself for anything asinine that may come from this person's lips. How do I know he will say something asinine? Just call it intuition. It rarely fails me. I am ready, pal. Hit me with it. And God, please help me to try to be loving and respectful even if he does not deserve it.

"So, your drummer tells me that you played a show last night at the heathen bar up the road. I want you all to know that my sister is a huge fan of yours, and now I have to tell her that you guys played a show there. Do you know the types of scumbags that hang out there? I am a Christian and so is my sister, but evidently you guys don't seem to care about your Christian witness at all. This is really disheartening and discouraging. I thought you guys were supposed to be a Christian band. How could you play a place like that?"

His eyes move around the inside of our RV, as he stands in our midst. No one is acknowledging his presence besides me, not our road manager, not our merch guy, not anyone from the band. He scans everyone. Randy is reading a copy of *Teen Vogue*, or something to that affect. Christian mechanic guy's eyes stop on the magazine, and he scoffs. Then he looks at our fridge, which has a picture of that group "T.A.T.U" on it—you know, the hokey Russian girl pop duo whose gimmick is pretending to be lesbians? His mouth curls into a snarl at the site of the picture of the two girls, who are embracing one another in the photo in a very PG manner. Then he sees our Olsen Twins poster, which is Logan's contribution to the aesthetic of the room. Needless to say, the guy grimaces once again when he sees it, even though it is an obvious joke, like all the other things he has just looked at.

I stare at his eyes, the emotion beginning to well up in me, seeing his ignorant wheels turning. Remember when I prayed a couple moments ago for the strength to be cool to this guy? I don't have it. He is trying to take away everything good, right, and just that we represent. Oh, but apparently he has more to say:

"Look at this place. How in the world can you guys even pretend to be believers with all the filth that is in here? I mean, this guy is reading a porn magazine. And look at your fridge. I get a very evil feeling being in here. You all are false prophets, and I can see that you do not care at all about presenting Christ to the world. My sister will be heartbroken when she hears this. I don't understand any of this. Don't you guys have anything to say for yourselves? You have lost supporters on this very day, and I hope you guys fail from here on out because you have turned your back on God."

I am currently still just staring at him, my jaw clenched, my lips pursed. I can do this. I know I can. I can handle it.

"The Bible tells us not to give the appearance of evil, and you guys call yourselves saved. You are going to have to answer for this for all eternity. You are leading people astray. I am ashamed to say that I actually told someone this last week about your band, because I thought you guys would be a good replacement in my friend's life for all the wretched music he was listening to. I guess I am going to have to go back to him and tell him I was wrong. God cannot use any of you for any good when you live like this. Your lives are being wasted—"

It just happens, and so quickly. Yet, despite the speed of the moment, I know I will be able to recall the dirty details oh-so-vividly for years to come. The first thing I remember feeling is the heat surging through my body, then turning to a flash of cold traveling first from my forehead, then down through my face, and finally darting through my midsection and appendages. Then, as if it was purely an autonomic reflex, my feet press into the floor, causing my body to straighten, erect, standing. Then my stomach muscles tighten along with my thighs as I launch from my seat, arms extended in a choking pose. I am reaching forward to wring this super-Christian mechanic's neck, once and for all. Luckily, Alex is quicker than he looks.

I come within approximately three inches of him before I am tackled by my drummer, who has undoubtedly just saved us thousands of dollars in would-be lawsuit losses. Funny how I would stake my life on the fact that this utterly righteous former Project 86 fan would try to sue our pants off in complete obedience to all his seemingly biblical ethics. That's just how these things pan out usually, wouldn't you agree? So, I am lying on my back with a two hundred-plus pound percussionist on top of me, screaming obscenities about how my mechanic friend should leave town along with his family and friends, reminiscent of a great scene in the movie *High Fidelity*. It all goes something like this:

"WHO INVITED YOU INTO OUR HOUSE IN THE FIRST PLACE, YOU MAGGOT! YOU HAVE NO BUSINESS COMING IN HERE AND TELLING US HOW WE SHOULD GO ABOUT WHAT WE DO! ARE YOU A COMPLETE RETARD, OR DO YOU JUST ALWAYS BARGE INTO STRANGERS' HOUSES AND CRITICIZE THEIR LIVES?! I WANT NOTHING TO DO WITH ANYTHING YOU STAND FOR!! DO YOU EVEN KNOW ME?! DO YOU EVEN KNOW MY LIFE?! DO YOU HAVE ANY IDEA HOW

MUCH PEOPLE LIKE YOU DESTROY WHAT WE DO? LEAVE THE COUNTRY AND TAKE YOUR FAMILY WITH YOU BEFORE I HUNT YOU ALL DOWN AND BURN DOWN YOUR HOMES!!"

Of course, I am yelling all of this on my back while Alex is pinning me down, so it looks slightly, if not completely, ridiculous. No matter. The dude is scared out of his mind and bolts from the RV with breakneck speed.

Now, I am not saying I am proud of the whole thing. In the end, you have your goals, your friends, your family, your faith—wherever it may lie. For me, I have an unending quest for some sense of fruit in everything I do, be it relationships, music, or otherwise. And when someone comes along with absolutely no respect or understanding for what I hold dear, I have to stand up and be counted. Period. Mr. Mechanic learned a valuable lesson on this very day, and for that, despite the means and err on my part, I am thankful. He will think twice, no matter his staunch observance to his supposed crusade, about barging into another man's home and attacking his living. That's something you just don't do, kids.

We have nothing if we don't first have respect for one another.

We have nothing if we don't first put ourselves in the other man's shoes.

So here we are, pages later, shows past, years under our belts. Gifts upon precious gifts. Wounds upon crucial disappointments. Show after show after show after show after show. I never planned to do what I do, nor did I ever plan that my little band would have the opportunity to make four albums, embark on national tours with some of the most successful acts in the land, meeting countless "stars" and remaining unimpressed in the process. I never even dreamed that I would ever hold a pen and sign another human being's T-shirt simply because something I created touched them. I never could have predicted that someone from a small town called Meadville, Pennsylvania, destined for a mediocre rural existence, would do something meaningful. And that's just it, in the end. Will there ever be a Project 86 *Behind The Music*? I doubt it. Will we even be remembered at all even a year after it is all said and done? Not by many. We will eventually be just another metal (or nu-metal, or hardcore, or whatever other label the categorical music media attaches) band that could have been "the next P.O.D. or Deftones or blahblahblah" if we would have just had that one hit song. It doesn't matter. Not to me. Not on this day. I want to say thanks to that kid Jeremy, wherever he is. Despite all his mistakes, I want to let the world know that his words, his honesty, changed me, once and for all, into someone that truly believes that honest music, honest art, saves lives. It will be all I need to look back, sagging chest tattoos, ear hair uncontrollable, bag for a belly, and say beyond all doubt that I was able to do something that mattered, even if I had to watch many of my peers get their gold and platinum plaques while I sat in the background watching.

I would also like to thank all the car-mechanic crusaders for showing me who not to be. You make it abundantly clear that I never want to be associated with you or your alleged cause. I don't care if the entire planet lumps us together into the same category. I know I am nothing like you. We may meet again on the other side. Then again, we may not. Either way, let it be known that your ignorance, your lack of discernment, your utter judgmentalism, does nothing but hinder those you think you are trying to save.

So, in the end …
You can have your platinum plaque.
You can have your Puritanical crusade.
You can have your major label deal.

Your hype.

Your gross commission.

Your A&R telling horrible jokes that you have to laugh at.

Your slot in afternoon rotation.

You can have your GMA nomination.

You can have your H3.

You can have your pick of the Band-Aid litter.

Your praise for polished stage banter.

Your rock club altar call.

Your cross-collateralization.

You can have your sixteen options and back catalogue rights.

You can have your catchy chorus.

You can have your 25 percent venue fee for T-shirts we sell so we can afford a place to sleep.

Your incessant need to call us Christian, heretical, calloused, has-been, or never-was.

Your indie-rock, spaz-core, screamo, or metal cred.

Your commitment to high fashion.

You can have your misspelled tour poster.

You can have your declining to tour with us because you think we aren't viable.

You can have your bad review with seven-syllable words you think make you sound clever.

Your condemning condescension when I compliment your record.

Your brohawk.

Your mediocre attempts at credibility.

You can have your dreds, your studs, your twelve-inch eyelets.

You can have your new T-shirt design with the stars and the cool shotgun logo.

You can have your in-store signings at 9 a.m.

Your bad demo that sounds like a less-talented version of Rage.

Your Afro.

Your cliché Asian tattoos.

You can have your failed attempts at sounding compelling in your bad poetry.

You can have your late royalty payments.

You can have your rickety touring van.

Your ability to quote 18 Visions lyrics.

Your desire to date my guitarist.

You can have your supposed friendship with Walter Schreifels.

You can have your sold out show at HOB Sunset.

You can have your secret thieving of my publishing advances.

Your envy of my apparent lack of dignity.

Your "art."

Your bass rig with seventy-four thousand preamps and space shuttle lights.

You can have your wigga adjectives.

You can have a tour with Linkin Park opening for you just before their ten million-plus record drops.

You can have your side-stage slot on Ozzfest.

Your voice lessons.

Your vocal chord nodules.

Your re-creation of yourself in your new promo photos complete with a Hitler hairdo.

You can have your tour stories from doing merch with Queens of the Stone Age.

You can have your name-dropping, stepping-on-all-those-in-your-way path to road success.

You can have your secret dissension.

Your passive-aggressive bandmates.

Your invitation to Fred Durst's dressing room, complete with "Nookie" dancers.

Your pound with Eminem.

Your near-date with Alyssa Milano.

You can have your half-million dollar, overproduced concept record which has no prayer of succeeding even if there are some real keeper songs on it.

Your suicidal girlfriend who influenced your first two records.

Your fickle, see-through attempt at social commentary.

Your invitation to tour with Marilyn Manson.

You can have your stalker letter, and believe me there are many.

You can have your CBGB T-shirt, friend, though you have no clue what it means.

You can have your leech female scenesters who talk so much yet contribute so little, besides more inspiration for songs about leech female scenesters, of course.

Your late tour support check, leaving you high and dry, fundless, in Omar, Kentucky, and without a hotel room.

Your tennis shoes with flames on the sides, which you think are somehow "cool," yet somehow many, many Midwesterners still buy your records.

You can have your dysfunctional, competitive relationship with your guitarist.

Your "dedicated" following of youngsters who would rather burn your music than buy it, thus jeopardizing your very existence.

Your deadly dancing circle of football players, endangering the rest of the audience.

Your post-show catharsis, when the whole world seems to be at your feet for just one evening.

You can have your industry of thieving elbow-rubbers and name-dropping hangers on.

You can have your dissenters who loved your "early stuff," but who have now dedicated themselves to ridiculing your band on your own band's online forum.

You can have your friends who only became your friends when you starting making a name for yourself.

Your less-than loyal product manager who threatens that perks like flights to New York City and seventy-five dollar dinners will all end if you don't start scanning more than fifteen hundred a week.

Your tour manager who stores cash in crumpled and disheveled clumps under his bunk on the bus.

Your late rent payment because your living expenses from the label somehow disappeared in the politics.

You can have your negligent bus driver who parks the bus in the wrong lane, nearly killing your bass player when he unknowingly steps off said bus into traffic.

You can have your strep throat, caused by shaking too many sweaty, grubby hands after a show in an attempt to be a "cool guy."

You can have your rash caused by sweaty exertion in unmentionable places.

Your CDs.

Your TSs.

Your SFs.

You can have your pre-show jitters.

You can have your hurry up and waits.

You can have your too-early load-in times.

Your early morning, rush-hour traffic, LAX flights when you should be flying out of Orange County.

Your "It is what it is's."

Your "Dinners on the label."

Your packaging deductions.

You can have your encouraging words from those who stuck by you when you haven't toured in a year.

You can have your "What happens on the mile stays on the miles."

You can have your frustrated girlfriends when you are out of town for weeks at a time.

Your rapidly dropping weight from having acid reflux, thus limiting your diet on the road to exactly three dishes: chicken, fish, and chicken with no lemon.

Your inability to talk for hours before the show because you blew it out the night before, which includes talking to long-lost family members who flew four hours to see your show for the first time in their lives.

Your drummer's disgusting, sweaty laundry which hangs all over your touring vehicle.

You can have the most beautiful experience on stage, at a summer festival in the rain.

You can have a wonderful conversation with an adorable fan who just wants you to know how much you have helped her through her day.

You can have a really bad hair *year* and have it captured in dozens of photos on dozens of websites.

Your shared microphone germs in clubs.

Your inability to afford the proper crew and gear to compete with the other bands on your level.

Your royalty check from SESAC that comes just in time for you to make your car payment.

You can have your first real show with a real band, making you feel like Superman.

You can have your first trip to Europe.

You can have girls screaming your name and even grabbing at your crotch at a random show in New Hampshire.

Your name on a marquis three thousand miles from home.

Your song on a random radio station in Nebraska (moment of silence).

Your entire career come crashing down because a record executive somewhere in a big-city high-rise decided he wants to commit their marketing dollars to The Donnas instead of your band.

You can have all this and more …

In the end, you can live much of this, see most of this, and be a witness to it all. In the end, you can take the high and lows, the ebbs and flows. You can add it up and throw it all together, and mix it in a caldron. And though on paper the answer is clear, you still will not listen.

In the end, I can scream until my eyes bulge, my blood clots, and the veins in my neck explode. In the end, I can write until I have arthritis so bad that my knuckles resemble kneecaps. And though it all makes perfect sense, you still will not pay attention.

In the end, all of the risk and all of the failure and all of the sleepless nights and all of the empty promises will not matter. In the end, all of the thieving managers and we-came-so-closes and we-almost-were-huge-but-oh-my-dear-son-the-big-one-got-aways will not matter. It just will not matter.

Why?

Because one kid will walk up to you at some random show in Maine when you are at your lowest, and he will tell you with tears in his eyes that you saved his life. And he will mean it. And you will be cut to the heart. And all the complaints in the world that you had not a few minutes prior will disappear. Because you will write that one song, that one chorus, that one note that is magical. Because in the end, when it is all said and done, you will come back home, if you are true, if you are real, if you really have been gifted to do what you are doing and God in heaven has set this task before you. Because in the end, when it is all over and you are lying on your deathbed with faded tattoos and a saggy yet supportive wife by your side, you will look back and know that you took the risk, you stepped out in faith. And you know what? You actually DID do something that mattered, even if it was only to a few people.

And though it was never, ever, glamorous, nor anything like what they told you it would be, one thing stands true. One thing and one thing only matters, above all else in the end. Nothing else matters in the whole world besides this one thing:

You did it all for the love. You did it all for THE LOVE.